Nita Mehta®

EGGL[...]

Cakes & Muffins

Nita Mehta

B. Sc. (Home Science); M. Sc. (Food and Nutrition), Gold Medalist

Nita Mehta®

EGGLESS
Cakes & Muffins

Snab Publishers Pvt Ltd
3A/3, Asaf Ali Road, New Delhi 110 002

Editorial and Marketing office
E-159, Greater Kailash II, New Delhi 110 048

Food Styling and Photography by Snab
Typesetting by National Information Technology Academy
3A/3, Asaf Ali Road, New Delhi 110 002

Recipe Development & Testing:
Nita Mehta Foods - R & D Centre
3A/3, Asaf Ali Road, New Delhi - 110002

ISBN 978-81-7869-323-1

4th Print 2017

Cover Designed by:

Printed in India at Pushpak Press Pvt. Ltd., New Delhi.

Distributed by :
NITA MEHTA BOOKS
3A/3, Asaf Ali Road, New Delhi - 02
Distribution Centre :
D16/1, Okhla Industrial Area, Phase-I,
New Delhi - 110020
Tel.: 26813199, 26813200
E-mail: nitamehta.mehta@gmail.com
Website: www.nitamehta.com

Contributing Writers :
Anurag Mehta
Tanya Mehta
Subhash Mehta
Editors :
Sangeeta
Sunita

Price: Rs. 295/-   US$ 12.95   UK£ 9.95

CONTENT

TINS AND PANS...

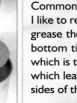

Round Loose Bottom Tin/Springform Tin

They really come into use when it is not possible to unmould a cake by inverting the tin. Common problem with a loose bottom tin is that sometimes the batter may leak while baking. I like to remove the base and cover it well with foil and then position it back into the tin. I then grease the foil and put the batter in the tin lined with foil. To remove the cake from a loose bottom tin, the loose bottomed tin with the cake in it is simply placed on a metal container which is taller in height than the tin, and the baking tin is simply pushed down from the edges, which leaves the cake along with the loose bottom base, free on top of the container and the sides of the tin fall down.

Round and Square Tins

A normal round tin is most commonly used. Available in different sizes - 11" (large), 9" (medium) and 5" (small). An 8" square tin can be used in place of a 9" round tin.

Ring Mould/Tin

This has a ring in the middle and is difficult to line with paper, therefore it should be greased very well, all along the insides, including the ring area. Used in orange chiffon cake, cappuccino cake, swirled ring cake etc.

Muffin Tray/Muffin Pan

Muffins and small mini cakes are baked in a tray with depressions or cups (usually 9 or 12) in which you pour the batter. The muffin tray may be lined with paper cups. It is not always necessary to line the muffin tray with paper cups. You can simply grease the tray without the paper cups and then dust each depression with flour.

Individual Muffin Tins

Small individual cake tins which are placed on the wire rack. These are slightly deeper than the cups of the muffin pan, so the ready muffins are slightly bigger when baked in small individual tins. Jumbo muffins are baked in these tins.

Loaf Tin

4½"x8½". Mainly used for tea time cakes, here we have used it for pineapple almond tea loaf, lemon loaf, black raisin cake etc.

LINING AND GREASING TINS...

Lining Tins

To line tin bases, place the tin on a piece of paper, draw around the base of tin, remove tin from paper and cut along the drawn line with a scissor. Lift the round piece of paper and position in base of pan. Grease the paper lined base and sides nicely with a brush or by hand.

Greasing

The tin is brushed with any regular cooking oil (should be flavourless and odorless). A pastry brush can be used for this or if not available, this can be done by hand also. The tin after greasing should be left to stand for 1 or 2 minutes. Any excess oil which has collected at the base, if at all, should be poured out. When paper is not used, it is good to dust the tin with flour after greasing.

USEFUL EQUIPMENT...

Kitchen Weighing Balance

This is used for weighing ingredients and is a very useful device in baking. A kitchen balance can weigh upto 2 kg or upto 5 kg, normally with smaller indications worked for every 10 gms in 2 kg balance or 25 gms in a 5 kg balance. This could vary machine to machine. Place the balance at eye level and the lever at 0 level before use. Available at most crockery and utensil stores.

Electric Beater

This is a hand held machine, used for beating or whisking, for eg: butter and sugar, eggs and sugar or as per the recipe. It aids in making cakes light and fluffy and should not be substituted with a hand blender or mixers and food processors. The beater is equipped with adjustable speeds – slow to very fast.

Wooden Spoons

These are used to mix batters gently. Even broad metal spoons can be used. With spoons, the flour can be folded in an upward and downward motion or simply mixed gently.

Rubber Spatula

These are like flat spoons with a squarish rubber end. These are so flexible that they help take out all the batter from the bowl when it has to be transferred to the baking tin.

Palette Knife

This is a long knife, either flexible or firm, with no sharp edges. It is rounded or square cut at the end. It is totally flat and is used to level cream or other icings on the cake for a neater finished look. The blade of the knife is immersed in iced water to level and spread cream icings on cake. In very cold weather, the blade can be dipped in hot water to spread icings like frostings which set too quickly.

Wire Rack

This is used in the oven, to place the tin and also after baking to cool the cake. Cake should not be cooled on a plate, because this prevents steam from escaping and makes the cake soggy.

WEIGHING OR MEASURING...

Kitchen Weighing Scale

Measuring Spoons & Cups

We recommend that you weigh your ingredients using a weighing scale where ever the weight is given. Cup measure used in the recipes is the measuring cup which holds 200 ml liquid. Larger cups which hold upto 240 ml liquid are also available. Always fill the cup and level it with a knife. Do not tap before leveling it. Since different capacity cups are available, it is always better to use the weighing scale for correct measurements. However well you might beat a cake, if the proportion of the ingredients is not accurate, you might get disappointed. So, invest in a weighing scale, measuring cups and measuring spoons. However, these are the conversions...

- I cup maida/flour .... = 115 gms
- I cup powdered sugar .... = 125 gms
- I cup granulated sugar .... = 175 gms
- I cup brown sugar .... = 135 gms
- I cup softened yellow butter .... = 180 gms
- I cup softened white butter................ = 150 gms
- I cup oil.. = 170 gms
- I cup cream .... = 200 gms
- I cup juice/sugar syrup........................ = 200 ml
- I table spoon (tbsp) .... = 15 ml/gms
- I tea spoon (tsp) .... = 5 ml/gms

HOW TO TEST CAKES...

You can follow basic rules as a guide to check the doneness of the cake. A cake is baked when it is:

- well risen and of a good colour and feels firm and springy when pressed with the finger tips
- a toothpick/cake tester remains clean after being inserted into the cake at the highest point but if it comes out with wet batter sticking to it this means the cake should bake a little longer.

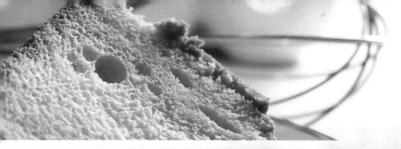

HANDY TIPS...

- All ingredients should be at room temperature for best results.
- Sift dry ingredients well, so that the mixture is aerated.
- Check expiry dates of ingredients, especially essences, baking powder and soda bi carb before use.
- Add essence to the fat because fat absorbs flavour readily.
- Always preheat oven to required temperature before baking.
- Use the correct size of the cake tin.
- A prepared cake mixture should go straight into the hot oven.
- Always bake in the centre of the oven.
- Do not beat the batter after the flour has been added or the finished cake will turn out heavy. Simply use a spoon to fold the flour in.

- When the recipe calls for 'beating', use an electric hand beater to beat the mixture till light and fluffy. If the recipe says to 'mix using a spoon', just mix all ingredients till well combined. Do not over mix or over beat.

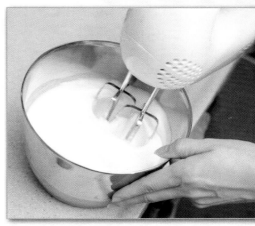

- Beating butter & sugar together is important. This is called creaming. The mixture should be beaten so well that it starts looking like whipped cream and becomes really fluffy and light.

- Sometimes the cake batter may appear too thick even though you may have measured the ingredients very carefully, as stated in the recipe. This happens because of the grade of flour that has been used. In such cases, you may conveniently add 2-4 tbsp of milk to make the batter softer.

- Fill cake tin only half to two-thirds full of batter, leaving enough space to rise.

- Tap filled cake tins gently on the kitchen platform to release any large air bubbles.

- Place tin in the centre of the oven, so that hot air can circulate around it.

- For even distribution of fruit and to avoid sinking of the dried fruit, mix fruit with a little flour before adding to the cake mixture.

- When cakes are removed from the oven, wait for 10-15 minutes before removing from the tin. Always remove cakes on a wire rack.

CAKE PROBLEMS...

Quality of Cake	Reasons - Any one or More

Heavy Cake
- Too little baking powder.
- Too much flour.
- Mixture (butter and sugar) not creamed enough.
- Flour mixed in too vigorously.
- Oven too slow (cake takes too long to get done).

A Dry Cake
- Too much baking powder or flour.
- Not enough fat or liquid.
- Too long in the oven.

A Sunken Cake
- Too much liquid.
- Too much baking powder or sugar.
- Too little flour.
- Oven door slammed or cake moved during baking.
- Taken out from the oven too soon.

A Peaked Cake
- Insufficient butter/oil or baking powder/soda.
- Too much flour.
- Oven temperature too high.

A Badly Cracked Top
- Oven too hot.
- Cake tin too small.
- Too much flour.
- Not enough liquid.

Fruit Sunk to the Bottom
- Fruit not properly dried and then coated with flour.
- Cake mixture too thin.
- Fruit added before adding the flour.

OVEN TEMPERATURES...

Always preheat oven to required temperature before baking.

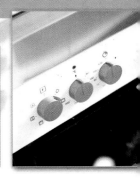

	°C	°F	Gas Mark
• Very cool	110	225	¼
• Cool	120	250	½
• Moderate	160-180	325-350	3-4
• Moderately Hot	190-200	375-400	5-6
• Hot	220-230	425-450	7-8
• Very Hot	240	475	9

BAKING IN A MICROWAVE...

A microwave oven on microwave mode cannot be used for baking any contents of this book. Only the convection mode of the microwave can be used for baking. So, only if your microwave has a convection mode, you can bake these cakes. When the microwave is on the convection mode, there are no microwaves travelling inside the microwave. Hence, all dishes and tins which go into the conventional OTG can very safely be used in the microwave. Metal cake tins, aluminium foil for covering or heat proof glass dishes work very well in the microwave when it is on the convection mode. To use the microwave oven for baking, set the needed temperature using the 'Convec button'. Press 'Start' to preheat the microwave oven. When the oven is heated to the desired temperature, it will give a beep. Do not press 'Stop'. Simply open the door, place the cake on the wire rack and close the door. Set only the 'time' needed to bake the cake, do not set the temperature. Press 'Start'. The cake now starts to get baked in the preheated oven at the set temperature and for the set time needed for baking.

Baking powder lying in the cupboard since many days...

Keep replacing baking powder and baking soda (*mitha soda*) after every 5-6 months. Before buying baking powder, check the manufacturing date. Baking powder stays good for a year only. To check if it is effective, put ½ tsp in a cup of hot water. If bubbles form, it is usable, if no bubbles, discard!

MELTING CHOCOLATE...

Cooking chocolate is used in a few recipes. Moisture and strong heat are the enemies of chocolate. To melt chocolate, make a proper double boiler, so that the steam does not reach the chocolate, as steam can give moisture to the melting chocolate.

Put chopped chocolate in a steel or heat proof bowl. Place bowl on a slightly smaller pan filled with 1" water, such that the chocolate bowl can sit on the pan of water without touching the water. Keep on very low heat and wait till the chocolate softens. Remove bowl from the pan of water and stir gently with a rubber spatula to melt chocolate completely. You can also melt chocolate in a microwave. Microwave 100 gms chocolate for 30-40 seconds only till soft. Stir with a rubber spatula to melt. If needed microwave for 30 seconds more.

MAKING A PAPER CONE...

Very handy for decorations.

1. Cut an 8" square piece of butter paper which is usually available in rolls like aluminium foil and cling wrap. Fold the square piece of paper to get a triangle. Cut on the fold to get 2 triangles.

2. Keep a triangle with the longest edge on top. Mark the centre of that edge. Place the paper triangle in your left hand, holding it with the thumb and fingers at the marked centre point. With the other hand holding the tip of the end, turn the paper once only at the centre point marked by your finger.

3. Lift the cone and wrap the far corner of the paper once around it, bringing all the points of the triangles together at the back. Adjust the tightness of the cone. Half fill the cone with icing. Fold open edges to close the bag. Cut a small hole for piping and squeeze gently.

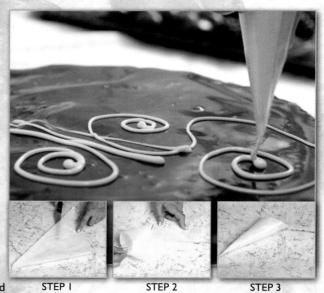

STEP 1   STEP 2   STEP 3

Tea Time Cakes

FRUIT CAKE

Vinegar and baking soda are used to create a fizzy batter that results in a moist, soft texture, with no taste of vinegar. Raisins and colourful candied fruit give tempting eye appeal.

INGREDIENTS

- 175 gms (1½ cups) flour (*maida*)
- ¾ tsp mixed spice (¼ tsp nutmeg, ¼ tsp cinnamon and ¼ tsp clove powder)
- 125 gms (1 cup) powdered sugar
- 100 gms (½ cup + 2 tbsp) yellow butter
- ½ cup milk, at room temperature
- 1½ tbsp white vinegar
- ½ tsp baking powder
- ½ tsp soda-bi-carb (*mitha soda*)
- 1 tsp vanilla essence
- 1 tbsp black raisins
- 4 tbsp chopped cashews
- 2 tbsp sliced glace cherries
- 2 tbsp candied fruit (red and yellow or green)

TOPPING

- 2 tbsp chopped cashews
- 2 tbsp sliced glace cherries
- 2 tsp flour (*maida*)

METHOD

1. Preheat oven to 190°C/355°F.
2. Prepare a 7½" x 4½" loaf cake tin.
3. Sift flour with mixed spice. Rub flour and butter together with the finger tips, till the mixture is crumbly. Do not over mix.
4. Add baking powder and sugar and mix lightly. Mix in raisins, nuts and fruit.
5. Divide milk into two parts. To one part which is at room temperature, add vinegar.
6. Warm the other part of milk slightly and add soda-bi-carb. Now mix both the milks together.
7. The milk will start foaming (bubbles appear). Add vanilla essence and this milk to the cake mix very quickly. Mix fast and well.
8. Scrape into the prepared tin. Level with a spatula. Mix the topping ingredients and sprinkle on the cake. Bake in preheated oven at 190°C/375°F for 20 minutes, then lower the temperature to 150°C/300°F for another 20 minutes.
9. When the cake is done, let it cool for 10 minutes before removing from the tin.

FRUIT CAKE

QUICK APPLE CAKE

QUICK APPLE CAKE

Serves 12

The fresh tart taste of green apples wrapped in spices and nuts – an evergreen fruity favourite.

MIX TOGETHER
- 190 gms (1¾ cups) flour
- 175 gms (1¼ cups) brown sugar
- 1 tsp baking soda (*mitha soda*)
- 1 tsp ground cinnamon (*dalchini*)
- 8 cloves (*laung*) ground (½ tsp)
- ¼ tsp grated nutmeg (*jaiphal*)

ADD LATER
- 1 cup butter-milk (¼ cup curd whisked and mixed with ¾ cup milk)
- ½ cup oil
- 1 tsp vanilla essence
- 2 tbsp rum or brandy, optional
- 1 cup chopped tart green apples
- 1 tbsp flour
- ½ cup roughly crushed peanuts/walnuts

TOPPING
- 1 tbsp brown sugar
- ½ tsp cinnamon (*dalchini*) powder
- 1 tbsp flour
- 1 tbsp chopped walnuts

METHOD
1. Mix flour, brown sugar, soda and the spices in a mixing bowl with a hand whisk till well mixed. Keep aside.
2. Add butter milk, oil, vanilla essence and rum. Stir till smooth.
3. Mix chopped apple with 1 tsp flour. Stir in apples and nuts. Mix lightly.
4. Scrape batter into a greased 7-8" round or square baking tin.
5. Mix ingredients of topping and sprinkle on the cake.
6. Bake in a preheated oven at 160°C for 45 minutes or till done.
7. Let the cake cool in the tin for 5 minutes and then remove from tin to a wire rack. Serve.

DARK CHOCOLATE CAKE

Chocolate lovers will appreciate this recipe for its quick simplicity — no beating needed, just mix the batter briskly and bake this yummy cake for any occasion.

INGREDIENTS

- 190 gms (1¾ cups) flour
- 180 gms (1½ cups) powdered sugar
- 1/3 cup + 1 tbsp cocoa powder
- 1 tsp baking soda (*mitha soda*)
- ½ tsp salt
- 1 cup cold refrigerated water
- ¼ cup oil
- 1 tbsp white vinegar
- 2 tsp vanilla essence
- ¼ cup soda water (a bottle of soda)
- 6-7" square tin - line bottom with paper and grease paper and sides

METHOD

1. Whisk flour, powdered sugar, cocoa powder, salt and baking soda in a bowl and keep aside.
2. Put cold water, oil, white vinegar and vanilla essence in a big mixing bowl.
3. Add flour, mix in 2-3 batches, folding gently with a wooden spoon each time. Do not over mix.
4. Pour ¼ cup soda water. Mix quickly.
5. Immediately transfer batter into the prepared 6-7" square tin. Bake at 170°C for 40 minutes. Check with tooth pick. To serve dust with icing sugar if you like.

DARK CHOCOLATE CAKE

LEMON LOAF

LEMON LOAF

A tongue-tingling taste with triple lemon extravagance – lemon juice, lemon rind and a lemony topping as well! Yogurt in the mix gives a soft and moist texture.

INGREDIENTS

- 1¼ cups yogurt
- 2 tbsp lemon juice
- rind of 1 lemon - cut lemon peel into very fine ½" long strips
- 90 gms (½ cup) salted butter
- 100 gms (¾ cup) powdered sugar
- 200 gms (1¾ cups + 1 tbsp) flour (*maida*)
- 2 tsp baking powder
- 1 tsp soda-bicarb
- 3 tbsp milk

TOPPING

- 3 tbsp sugar
- 2 tbsp lemon juice
- 1 tsp lemon rind
- a drop of yellow colour

METHOD

1. Line a 8" x 4" loaf tin with paper. Grease paper and sides.
2. Preheat oven to 190°C/375°F.
3. Peel one firm lemon as thinly as possible with a sharp knife, peeling only the upper yellow skin & leaving the white pith beneath. Shred the peel into very thin ½" long strips to get lemon rind.
4. Sieve flour, baking powder and soda-bi-carb together. Keep aside.
5. Beat sugar and butter very well. Mix lemon peel.
6. Mix yogurt and lemon juice and keep aside.
7. To the beaten sugar and butter, fold in sieved flour alternately with yogurt and lemon juice mixture. Mix. Do not over mix or beat. Add milk and mix gently.
8. Put immediately in the greased tin & bake in the preheated oven at 375°F/190°C for 30 minutes or till the cake is done.
9. The cake is very soft, so after removing from the oven, let it cool in the tin for 10 minutes and then remove to a wire rack. Keep aside.
10. For the topping, heat sugar, lemon rind and lemon juice over low heat, stirring continuously, till the sugar dissolves. Add a drop of yellow colour.
11. Pierce top of the cake with a fork and pour the prepared topping on top of the cake. Cool the cake uncovered, at least for 2 hours before cutting.

MALAI CAKE

The thick cream on top of boiled, cooled milk is the base of the batter for this rich and luscious cake – impress your guests!

INGREDIENTS

- 225 gms (2 cups) flour (*maida*)
- 255 gms (1¾ cups) caster or powdered sugar
- 1 cup thick *malai* (milk topping)
- 2 tsp vanilla essence
- few drops of lemon yellow colour, optional
- 1 tsp baking powder, ¼ tsp soda-bi-carb (*mitha soda*)
- 1 cup cold milk

METHOD

1. Take malai and caster sugar in a bowl and mix well with light hand or else the butter would come out of the malai.
2. Sieve the flour, baking powder and the soda 2-3 times and keep aside.
3. Gradually add half milk and half flour mixture to malai and keep stirring to mix.
4. Add the remaining mixture and stir well to mix.
5. Add the vanilla essence and the colour and lightly stir again once.
6. Line an 8" cake tin with paper. Grease paper and sides.
7. Transfer the batter into it.
8. Bake in a preheated oven at 180°C for 40 minutes.

CHOCOLATE COLA CAKE

This amazing cola-flavoured cake can be served with a dark & creamy chocolate topping that no one can resist!

INGREDIENTS

- 1 tin (400 gms) condensed milk
- 6 tbsp powdered sugar
- 125 gms butter
- 250 ml or 1 ¼ cups aerated cola drink (pepsi, coke)
- 5 tbsp cocoa powder
- 225 gms (2 cups) flour (*maida*)
- 2 tsp baking powder
- 1 tsp soda-bicarb (*mitha soda*)

METHOD

1. Preheat the oven to 150°C/300°F. Line a 10-11" cake tin with paper. Grease paper and sides.
2. Mix butter, sugar and condensed milk in a mixing bowl. Beat well.
3. Sift flour, cocoa, soda-bicarb and baking powder together.
4. Add flour gradually to the condensed milk and butter mixture, mixing with a spoon.
5. Add cola and mix well. Immediately transfer to the prepared tin. Bake in a preheated oven at 150°C/300°F for 60 minutes or till done. If a knife inserted in the centre of the cake comes out clean, remove from oven. Remove from tin after 5-7 minutes.

CHOCOLATE TOPPING

You can enjoy the above cake plain or enhance it further by pouring this quick and simple chocolate topping on it.

INGREDIENTS

- 200 gms cream, preferably Amul
- 200 gms dark cooking chocolate - chopped (2 cups)
- 2 tbsp sugar, 1 tbsp butter

METHOD

1. For chocolate topping, heat cream with sugar in a heavy bottom pan on low heat till it becomes hot. Add chocolate to it. Mix nicely to remove any lumps. Remove from fire when almost melted and stir to a smooth consistency. Add butter and mix well. Let it cool to room temperature. Keep cake on a rack. Place a plate under the rack. Pour the prepared icing on the cake and tilt it to cover the sides also.

ORANGE CHIFFON CAKE

*This elegant cake is generously saturated with orange squash, orange rind, and orange marmalade —
from base, to filling, to frosting.*

ORANGE CHIFFON CAKE

- 200 gms (1¾ cups + 1 tbsp) flour
- 1½ tsp baking powder
- ¾ tsp soda-bi-carb (*mitha soda*)
- 135 gms (¾ cup) butter - softened
- 115 gms (1 cup less 1 tbsp) powdered sugar
- ¾ cup milk
- 6 tbsp orange squash - undiluted or
  4 tbsp orange crush mixed with
  2 tbsp water

ORANGE FILLING

- 45 gms (¼ cup) yellow butter
- ½ cup icing sugar - sifted
- 1 tbsp orange rind
- 2 tbsp orange marmalade
- 2-3 drops lemon juice

ORANGE FROSTING

- 60 gms unsalted butter
- 1½ tbsp milk
- ½ tsp orange essence
- a pinch of orange colour
- 125 gms (1¼ cups) icing sugar
- 2-3 drops lemon juice

METHOD

1. For the orange chiffon cake, grease an 9" ring mould. Sieve the flour, baking powder and the soda-bi-carb. Beat butter and sugar till light and fluffy. Add the milk and orange squash. Mix with a spoon. Add flour and mix gently with a wooden spoon. Transfer to the prepared cake tin. Bake at 180°C/350°F for 25 minutes till golden and the cake shrinks from the sides of the tin. Let it cool before removing from the tin as the cake is very soft when hot.

2. For the orange filling, place a 1" piece of orange peel on flat surface with the white pith facing upwards. Take out orange rind by scraping away the white pith. Cut peel very finely into thin strips to get rind. Beat butter and sugar till light and fluffy. Add the orange marmalade and rind and mix gently.

3. Cut the cake into 2 round pieces. Place one piece on a big serving platter. Spread orange filling on the cut surface and invert the other piece of cake on it to cover.

4. For orange frosting, melt butter with milk on low heat in a saucepan. Remove from fire when the butter melts. Add colour and essence to it. Add lemon juice and icing sugar. Beat with an electric beater for 2-3 minutes until smooth. Pour warm icing on the cake on the top and let the icing fall on the sides. Cover the inner sides completely with frosting. Keep aside to set.

ORANGE CHIFFON CAKE

BLACK RAISIN LOAF WITH
LEMON FROSTING

BLACK RAISIN LOAF WITH LEMON FROSTING

Serves 8

This cake batter is made with sugar syrup. Utterly delicious with or without the lemon frosting.

INGREDIENTS

- 150 gms (1 cup less 2 tbsp) sugar
- 1 cup water
- ¼-½ cup black raisins or golden raisins
- 45 gms (¼ cup) yellow butter
- ¼ tsp ground cloves (*laung*)
- 190 gms (1¾ cups) sifted flour
- ½ tsp baking powder
- ½ tsp soda bicarb (*mitha soda*)

LEMON FROSTING (ICING)

- 1¼ cups confectioners sugar
- 60 gms unsalted butter
- 1½ tbsp water
- 1 tsp lemon essence
- 2-3 drops of lemon juice
- a drop of yellow colour

METHOD

1. Combine sugar, water, raisins, butter and ground cloves in a pan. Bring to a boil on low heat for the sugar to dissolve. Remove from fire. Let mixture cool.
2. Sift flour, baking powder and soda.
3. Fold in the flour with a wooden spoon. Do not over mix.
4. Turn batter out into a 6-7" loaf tin that has been lined with paper and greased. Bake in a preheated oven at 180°C for 35 minutes. Allow to cool before frosting.
5. For lemon frosting, melt butter with milk on low heat in a saucepan. Remove from fire when the butter melts. Add lemon juice, just a drop of colour and essence to it. Add icing sugar. Beat with an electric beater for 2-3 minutes until smooth. Pour warm icing on the cake on the top and tap cake lightly to coat thinly and let the icing fall on the sides and coat the sides as well. Keep aside to set.

Note:

For children, you can also make cut outs of animals from marzipan paste as given on page 45 and decorate on the frosted cake.

SWIRLED RING CAKE

Serves 8

The swirling colours look very professional – but so easy to do when you follow these clear instructions.

INGREDIENTS

- 125 gms (1 cup + 2 tbsp) flour
- 150 gms (1 cup) powdered sugar
- ½ cup yogurt
- 75 gms (½ cup) softened white butter
- 1 tsp baking powder
- ½ tsp soda bicarb (*mitha soda*)
- 1 tsp vanilla essence
- 2-3 tbsp milk, if needed

FOR SWIRL

- 2 tbsp cocoa powder
- 1 tbsp icing sugar
- 2 tbsp water

METHOD

1. Grease a 6" ring tin. Dust with flour.
2. Sieve flour, soda and baking powder together.
3. Beat white butter with an electric beater till soft and fluffy.
4. Add yogurt and beat again.
5. Add sugar gradually and beat. Add vanilla essence.
6. Fold in flour gently with wooden or metal spoon to get a soft dropping consistency. Add 2-3 tbsp milk if the batter appears very thick.
7. For the swirl, mix cocoa, icing sugar and water to thick paste in a small bowl.
8. Add this chocolate paste to cake mixture with a spoon and gently swirl with another spoon to make a marble effect. Do not use the same spoon for marbling and also do not mix uniformly. Both vanilla and chocolate mixture should show separately as marble effect.
9. Pour mixture into the prepared tin and bake in a preheated oven at 180°C for 25 minutes.
10. Insert skewer or knife in the cake. If it comes out clean, remove tin from oven. Keep aside for 5 minutes before unmoulding it. Loosen the inner and outer edges with a knife. Transfer to a wire rack. Let it cool.

STEP 8

SWIRLED RING CAKE

CAPPUCCINO CAKE

CAPPUCCINO CAKE

Serves 10-12

This is an excellent cake for small or large gatherings with or without the proverbial hot cup of cappuccino!! Can also be served as a sophisticated dessert with ice cream, if you wish.

INGREDIENTS

- 140 gms (1¼ cups) flour (*maida*)
- 30 gms (½ cup) cocoa powder
- 1 tsp baking powder
- ½ tsp soda-bi-carb (*mitha soda*)
- ¾ cup yogurt
- 150 gms (1¼ cup) powdered sugar
- ½ cup oil
- 3 tsp coffee powder mixed in 1 tbsp hot water
- 1 tsp vanilla essence
- 3 tbsp milk
- a big ring mould (8" diameter)

COFFEE SYRUP

- 2 tsp coffee powder
- ¼ cup brown sugar
- ¼ cup water

TO DECORATE

- 1 cup tinned cherries
- 4 dry, ready to eat apricots

STEP 1

METHOD

1. Grease a big (8-9" diameter) ring with oil, using a brush. Dust with cocoa.
2. Sift flour, baking powder, soda and cocoa powder together.
3. Combine coffee and hot water.
4. Beat yogurt and sugar to mix well. Add coffee mix and essence.
5. Add oil very gradually, while beating continuously.
6. Fold in sifted flour mixture with wooden spoon gently. Add 3 tbsp milk. Mix gently.
7. Pour mixture into the prepared tin. Bake in preheated oven at 160°C for 50 minutes. Insert a skewer or knife. If it comes out clean remove cake from oven. After 5 minutes transfer cake to the wire rack.
8. For the coffee syrup, combine sugar and water. Boil and stir over low heat till sugar dissolves. Remove from fire. Add coffee and let it cool. Soak cake with this coffee syrup.
9. Serve as it is or fill the centre hollow with cherries and place 4 apricots on top.

APPLE OAT CAKE

Oats and whole wheat flour make a healthy cake with the happy flavours of apples and cinnamon.

INGREDIENTS

- ½ tin condensed milk (200 gms)
- 50 gms (½ cup) oats
- 15 almonds - crushed roughly
- 25 gms (¼ cup) whole wheat flour (*atta*)
- 1 tsp baking powder, ½ tsp soda-bi-carb (*mitha soda*)
- ½ tsp cinnamon powder
- ½ cup oil
- 1 tsp vanilla essence
- 1 red apple - finely chopped with the peel, 2 tbsp flour

METHOD

1. Line with paper a small 6-7" round cake tin. Grease well.
2. Sift wheat flour with baking powder, baking soda and ½ tsp cinnamon powder.
3. Add oat and crushed almonds.
4. Beat condensed milk very well. Add essence. Mix well.
5. Add oil and beat.
6. Add flour mixture gradually and mix gently with a wooden spoon.
7. Sprinkle flour on the apples and mix well. Fold chopped apples into the batter with a spatula.
8. Transfer batter to the prepared tin. Bake in a pre-heated oven at 180°C/300°G for 40-45 minutes.

Muffins & Cup Cakes

DARK CHOCO CHIP MUFFINS

Makes 6-7

Buttermilk lifts the batter for these moist muffins while chocolate chips slowly melt into dark pools of seduction.

INGREDIENTS

- 90 gms (¾ cup) flour
- 20 gms (¼ cup) cocoa
- ½ tsp baking powder
- ¼ tsp soda-bi-carb (*mitha soda*)
- 75 gms (½ cup + 1 tbsp) powdered sugar
- 65 gms (1/3 cup) yellow butter
- 1 cup buttermilk (mix ¾ cup milk and ¼ curd)
- ½ tsp vanilla essence
- ¼ cup chocolate chips

TOPPING

- 2 tbsp chocolate chips

METHOD

1. Sift flour, cocoa, baking powder and soda. Keep aside.
2. Beat butter and sugar till soft and fluffy. Add essence and beat again.
3. Add 2 tbsp flour mixture and a little butter milk to the butter-sugar mixture. Fold them with a wooden spoon. Add the remaining flour and butter milk also in batches.
4. Fold chocolate chips into the muffin mix, swirling it just once or twice. Do not mix too much.
5. Grease muffin cups and line them with paper. Transfer the mixture in cups, filling them about ¾ full. Put water in the remaining cups of the muffin pan. Put some chips on top. Tap lightly.
6. Bake at 180°C until done (when tested with toothpick) for about 25 minutes. Some times the muffins may appear slightly wet when tested with a tooth pick. This may be due to the chips present in the muffins. Do not over bake. They will dry up on cooling.

ALMOND JUMBO MUFFINS

Tart sweet orange marmalade wakes up the senses while almonds give crunchy satisfaction.

INGREDIENTS

- 150 gms (1¼ cup) powdered sugar
- 2 cups buttermilk (mix 1½ cup milk and ½ cup yogurt), approx.
- 90 gms (½ cup) yellow butter
- 225 gms (2 cups) flour
- 1 tsp baking powder
- ½ tsp soda-bi-carb (*mitha soda*)
- 1 tsp orange essence

SWIRL LATER

- ½ cup orange marmalade

TOPPING

- 3-4 tbsp flaked almonds

METHOD

1. Sift flour, baking powder and soda. Keep aside.
2. Beat butter and sugar till soft and fluffy. Add essence and beat again.
3. Add 2 tbsp flour mixture and a little buttermilk. Fold them with a wooden spoon. Add the remaining flour and buttermilk also in batches. Add just enough butter milk to get a soft dropping consistency.
4. Whisk marmalade lightly but do not make it smooth. Fold marmalade into the muffin mix, swirling it just once or twice. Do not mix too much.
5. Grease individual muffin cups. Dust them with flour. Pour the mixture in them, filling them about ¾ full.
6. Top with almond flakes. Press lightly.
7. Bake at 180°C until done (when tested with toothpick) for about 25 minutes. Remove from oven. Let them cool in the tin before unmoulding. Serve.

FROSTED ALPHABET CUP CAKES

Kid-sized and kid-friendly – these colourful cup cakes are a little child's dream.

INGREDIENTS

- 115 gms (1 cup) flour
- 100 gms (¾ cup) powdered sugar
- ½ cup yogurt
- 75 gms (½ cup) softened white butter
- 1 tsp vanilla essence
- 1 tsp baking powder
- ½ tsp soda-bi-carb (*mitha soda*)
- ¼ cup milk

COVERING ICING

- 60 gms unsalted butter
- 1½ tbsp water or milk
- 125 gms (1¼ cups) icing sugar
- 1 tsp vanilla essence
- 1-2 drops lemon juice
- a few drops of green colour
- 1 tbsp cocoa
- silver balls, hundred thousand balls or other cake sprinklers

METHOD

1. For the cup cakes, line a muffin pan (tray) with paper cups.
2. Sieve flour, soda and baking powder together.
3. Beat white butter and essence with an electric beater till soft and fluffy.
4. Add yogurt and beat again. Add sugar gradually and beat.
5. Fold in flour gently with a wooden or metal spoon.
6. Add milk and stir gently.
7. Spoon mixture into lined cups, filling them ¾ only. Bake at 180°C for 20-25 minutes till golden and firm on the top. Keep aside to cool. Remove paper cups.
8. For covering icing, melt butter with milk on low heat in a sauce pan. Remove from fire. Add sugar, lemon juice and essence to it. Beat with an electric hand beater for 2-3 minutes until smooth and of a thick pouring consistency.
9. Remove half of the icing in a separate bowl. Add cocoa to the portion in the bowl and beat well to get a chocolate frosting. If the frosting appears too thick to pour, add 1-2 tsp hot water and mix again. Pour warm icing with a tbsp on four cakes and tap cake lightly. Sprinkle silver balls or other sprinklers.
10. To the remaining portion of frosting, add lemon juice, green colour and mix with a spoon. Warm the icing in a microwave for 5-10 seconds if it has turned thick and cannot be poured properly. Pour on the remaining cup cakes.
11. Replace the paper cups.
12. Transfer the remaining green and chocolate frostings in small butter paper cones. Write the first alphabet of the names of children, green alphabet on chocolate cake and chocolate alphabet on a green cake.

FROSTED ALPHABET CUP CAKES

QUICK CUP CAKES

QUICK CUP CAKES

Make a proper round cake and cut small cakes with a cookie cutter from it. Ice them beautifully with chocolate or any other butter icing.

INGREDIENTS

- 1 recipe vanilla cake or malai cake, page 55 or page 20, see note
- some orange marmalade or jam to sandwich the cup cakes
- gems, sugar candies for decoration

BUTTER ICING

- 75 gms (½ cup) unsalted white butter, softened
- 150 gms (1½ cups) icing sugar - sifted
- 1 tbsp boiling water
- 1 tsp vanilla essence
- 2 drops lemon juice
- 1-2 tbsp cocoa powder

METHOD

1. Prepare 1 kg cake as given on page 55. If making the malai cake, double the recipe and bake in a bigger tin to get 8 cup cakes. You can also buy ready made sponge cake from a bakery. Let the cake cool.

2. Cut the cake with a cookie cutter into small cakes. Cut each cake into 2 pieces. Spread some jam or marmalade on a piece and place the other piece of cake on it. Press lightly to stick. See that the height of all the cakes looks the same. Keep aside covered.

3. For the vanilla icing, beat the butter with an electric beater until light and fluffy. Gradually add the icing sugar, beating well after each addition. Add the water and beat well. Add essence. Divide icing into 2 parts. To one part add cocoa powder, adding enough to get a nice chocolate colour. If need be add 1-2 tsp hot water. Put in a piping bag fitted with a star nozzle and pipe round circles on 4 cakes, starting from the edge to the centre. Make a swirl when you reach the centre. Repeat the same with white icing on the remaining cakes.

4. Arrange coloured sweets and gems on the cake.

Note:

You can also buy plain muffins and convert them into beautifully iced muffins.

JAM MUFFINS

In this recipe, mixed fruit jam is lightly swirled into the batter – a speedy treat for the hungry young crowd.

INGREDIENTS

- 75 gms (½ cup) brown sugar
- 1 cup buttermilk (mix ¾ cup milk and ¼ yogurt)
- 65 gms (1/3 cup) yellow salted butter
- 115 gms (1 cup) flour (*maida*)
- 1 tbsp cocoa powder
- ½ tsp baking powder
- ¼ tsp soda-bi-carb (*mitha soda*)
- ½ tsp vanilla essence

ADD LATER

- ¼ cup mixed fruit jam or any flavour

TOPPING

- 6-8 glace cherries - sliced

METHOD

1. Sift flour, cocoa, baking powder and soda. Keep aside.
2. Beat butter and sugar till soft and fluffy. Add essence and beat again.
3. Add 2 tbsp flour mixture and a little buttermilk. Fold them with a wooden spoon. Add the remaining flour and buttermilk also in batches.
4. Whisk jam lightly but do not make it smooth. Fold jam into the muffin mix, swirling it just once or twice. Do not mix too much.
5. Line and grease a muffin pan. Transfer the mixture in cups, filling them about ¾ full. Put water in the remaining empty cups of the muffin pan if any. Arrange slices of glace cherry on top and press lightly.
6. Bake at 180°C until done (when tested with toothpick) for about 25 minutes.

JAM MUFFINS

CHOCO CHIP BUTTERFLIES

CHOCO CHIP BUTTERFLIES

A slice from the top of the muffin is shaped into butterfly wings to delight young fans.

CHOCOLATE CHIP MUFFINS

- 190 gms (1¾ cups) flour (*maida*)
- ½ tsp baking powder
- ½ tsp soda-bi-carb
- 125 gms (2/3 cup) yellow butter
- 115 gms (1 cup less 1 tbsp) powdered sugar
- 1 cup milk, at room temperature
- 1½ tbsp white vinegar
- 1 tsp vanilla essence
- ½ cup chocolate chips

TO MAKE BUTTERFLIES

- ¾ cup (150 ml) cream
- 2 tbsp icing sugar
- 2-3 red glace cherries

STEP 7

STEP 8

STEP 9

STEP 10

METHOD

1. Rub flour, baking powder and butter together with the finger tips, till the mixture is crumbly. Do not over mix. Add sugar and mix lightly. Mix chocolate chips and vanilla essence.

2. Divide milk into two parts. To one part which is at room temperature, add vinegar. Warm the other part of milk slightly and add soda-bi-carb. Now mix both the milks together.

3. The milk will start foaming (bubbles appear). Add this to the cake mix very quickly. Mix fast and well.

4. Transfer mixture to muffin cups. Bake in preheated oven at 190°C/375°F for 10 minutes, then lower the temperature to 150°C/300°F for another 10 minutes.

5. When the muffins are done, let them cool for 10 minutes before removing from the tin. Turn onto wire rack to cool completely.

6. If using tetra pack Amul cream, do not shake. Open and discard liquid which settles at the bottom. Beat thick cream and icing sugar until soft peaks form. Cut each cherry into 4-6 slices. Keep cream and cherries aside.

7. Using point of a small knife, cut shallow small rounds from top of cakes.

8. Cut rounds in half.

9. Spoon 1 tbsp cream into holes in the cakes. Spread some cream on the outside of the hole also.

10. Place halved cake tops at an angle on the cream.

11. Arrange cherries in middle to resemble butterflies. Refrigerate till serving time.

MOLTEN CHOCO CUP CAKES

Makes 8-9

These cupcakes are flavoured with orange squash & filled with melted creamy chocolate. Serve warm. Indulge yourself and your youngster's friends!

INGREDIENTS

- 190 gms (1¾ cups) flour (*maida*)
- 1½ tsp baking powder
- ¾ tsp soda-bi-carb (*mitha soda*)
- 75 gms (1 tbsp less than ½ cup) yellow salted butter - softened
- 100 gms (¾ cup) powdered sugar
- ½ cup milk
- ½ cup orange squash or orange crush

CHOCOLATE FILLING

- ¾ cup (150 gms) cream, preferably Amul cream
- 100 gms dark cooking chocolate - cut into tiny pieces (1 cup)

METHOD

1. Sieve flour, baking powder and soda-bi-carb.
2. Beat butter and sugar till fluffy.
3. Add half of the flour and half of the milk. Mix well and add the remaining plain flour. Add remaining milk. Beat very well till light and fluffy.
4. Add orange squash or crush and mix to get a soft dropping consistency. Add 1-2 tbsp milk if the batter appears too thick. Do not beat too much.
5. Line a muffin pan (tray) with paper cups. Spoon mixture into them filling them ¾ only. Bake at 180°C for 25-30 minutes till golden and firm on the top. Keep aside.
6. For filling, heat cream in a small heavy bottomed pan, on low heat. Add chocolate and heat stirring continuously for a minute, till chocolate melts and you get a smooth paste. Keep aside to come to room temperature and become slightly thick.
7. Cut out a small circle from the bottom of each muffin. Keep the cap aside. Scoop out the cake slightly. Fill with chocolate filling. Replace the cap again to close the cup cake. Keep aside till serving time. Do not refrigerate.
8. To serve, put the muffins on a serving platter which should be micro-proof. Warm in a microwave for 10-15 seconds. Serve.

MOLTEN CHOCO CUP CAKE

MARZIPAN CUP CAKES

MARZIPAN CUP CAKES

Learn the professional way to make almond paste (marzipan) decorations & add your own creative touch.

CUP CAKES

- ½ tin condensed milk (200 gms)
- ¼ cup milk, approx.
- ½ cup oil
- 4 tbsp powdered sugar
- 175 gms (1½ cups) flour (*maida*)
- ¼ cup almonds - chopped finely
- ½ tsp soda-bicarb (*mitha soda*)
- 1 tsp baking powder
- 1 tsp vanilla essence

MARZIPAN TOPPING

- 1/3 cup almonds - blanched
- 1/3 cup icing sugar
- 2½ tbsp fine grain sugar
- 3 tbsp water
- 1 tsp liquid glucose (microwave for a few seconds if hard)
- different colours - raspberry red, blue, green, yellow
- 1-2 tbsp chopped chocolate - melted for eyes of animals

METHOD

1. For the cup cakes, sift flour with soda-bicarb and baking powder. Add chopped almonds. Keep aside. Mix sugar and milk maid. Beat till light. Add oil. Beat well to mix. Add half of the flour and half the milk. Mix gently with a wooden spoon. Add essence. Add the remaining flour and the milk, mixing gently to get a thick pouring batter. Pour batter in a greased muffin pan. Bake for 20 minutes in a preheated oven at 150°C.

2. For the topping, put almonds in 1 cup water and microwave for 1-2 minutes. Slip the skins off and pat dry with a paper napkin. Grind almonds and icing sugar in a grinder to a fine powder. Leave in the grinder till sugar syrup is ready.

3. Cook grain sugar and water is a small flat pan to a 2½ string (soft ball stage) consistency. Check a drop of syrup in a bowl of water. It forms a soft ball. Add liquid glucose to syrup. Mix.

4. Remove syrup from fire and immediately add hot syrup to almond-sugar mix in the grinder. Grind all together to a paste. Remove marzipan to the kitchen platform. Knead for about 2-3 minutes till a nice pliable dough is ready. Divide into portions and colour as you like. Always keep the marzipan dough covered, wrapped in cling wrap.

5. Roll out the dough on the kitchen platform dusted with icing sugar thinly. Using a cookie cutter, first cut out a round and place on the cup cake. Press lightly. Then roll out a different coloured dough and cut out animals etc from it. Stick using a little water on the cakes. Dip a tooth pick in melted chocolate and make eyes if you like.

BLUEBERRY MUFFINS

Makes 8

Blueberry jam is used to recreate the taste of fresh-picked mountain blueberries. Make a slit on top of the baked muffin, fill with jam and bake for a few more minutes.

INGREDIENTS

- 200 gms (1¾ cups) flour (*maida*)
- 115 gms (1 cup less 1 tbsp) powdered sugar
- 1½ tsp baking powder
- ¾ tsp soda-bi-carb (*mitha soda*)
- 90 gms (½ cup) salted butter - softened
- 1 tsp vanilla essence
- ¾ cup milk mixed with ¼ cup yogurt (buttermilk)
- 3-4 tbsp blueberry jam

METHOD

1. Mix the flour, baking powder and the soda-bi-carb.
2. Mix milk with yogurt to get butter milk. Keep aside.
3. Beat butter in a mixing bowl. Add sugar and beat till light and creamy. Add essence. Add half of the flour and half of the buttermilk and fold with a spatula. Add the remaining flour and buttermilk to get a lumpy batter. Fold till just blended. Do not over mix.

STEP 6

4. Line a muffin pan (tray) with greased paper cups.
5. Spoon mixture into them filling them ¾ only. Bake at 180°C for 20 minutes.
6. Make a slit on the cooked muffin with a knife and insert 1 tsp jam in each. Bake for 5-7 minutes more. Remove muffins from tin after 5 minutes.

CARROT & BANANA MUFFINS

The secret for making this classic muffin batter is to leave it lumpy – do not over mix. Pureed bananas, grated carrots, and raisins make a delectable taste and texture combination.

INGREDIENTS

- 85 gms (¾ cup) whole wheat flour (*atta*)
- 85 gms (¾ cup) flour (*maida*)
- 1½ tsp baking powder
- ¾ tsp soda-bi-carb (*mitha soda*)
- 1 cup grated carrots
- 3 tbsp raisins
- 90 gms (½ cup) yellow salted butter - softened
- 1 tsp vanilla essence
- 150 gms (1 cup + 2 tbsp) powdered sugar
- 2 ripe bananas - chop and then mash with a fork (1 cup)
- 1/3 cup milk, approx.

METHOD

1. Sieve the flours, baking powder and the soda-bi-carb.
2. Add carrots and raisins to the flour. Keep aside
3. Beat butter, essence and sugar till light and fluffy. Remove the beaters.
4. Add half of the flour and mix well with a spatula. Add the remaining flour and mix to get a thick lumpy batter. Do not over mix. Just mix enough to moisten the dry ingredients.
5. Add mashed bananas and fold to mix. Add just enough milk slowly to get a thick dropping batter.
6. Line a muffin pan (tray) with paper cups. Spoon mixture into them, filling them ¾ full. Tap lightly. Bake at 160°C for 25-30 minutes till golden on the top.

Party Cakes

PIPING DESIGNS

I. SIMPLE STARS

Hold the piping bag or gun fitted with a star nozzle vertically and press a simple star. Stop pressing and lift the bag sharply. The bag should be held absolutely upright. Equal pressure should be applied while squeezing to get equal sized stars.

2. STAR BORDER

Same as for simple stars in #1, but make stars one after the other without leaving space in between.

3. COMMA BORDER

Pipe commas without gap with star nozzle.

4. SWIRLS

Same as for simple stars in #1, but press in a circular motion, stop pressing and lift sharply.

5. SHELL BORDER

Hold bag fitted with star nozzle at 45° angle, squeeze to make the 2nd shell on top of the tail. Repeat.

6. SHELL FLOWERS

Pipe a central elongated shell, then pipe a smaller curved shell on the left and on the right, overlapping both left and right tails on the center tail.

7. SIMPLE WRITING

Use a plain piping nozzle or paper cone with a small hole and pipe desired script or message with cream, melted chocolate or jam.

HANDLING CREAM

Creams differ in the amount of fat content and thus need to be handled accordingly. We have worked with 3 kinds of cream that are easily available and here we tell you how each one is handled to get the best results. Tetrapack creams have a long shelf life, so cakes iced with these stay well for a week or sometimes even more, whereas the cakes iced with fresh dairy cream need to be consumed within a day. When you beat cream for using in cakes, there are mainly 3 different stages of the thickness or consistency of the cream that is needed. For...

1. Spreading inside the cake...

Beat cream till thick and has a soft dropping consistency.

2. Topping the cake...

Beat further till cream is more firm and reaches a soft peak consistency. Check the icing by lifting the beater blades. If it forms soft peaks then its ready to be topped on cakes. When lifted from the bowl with a spatula the peak will stand up but droop over slightly at the tip.

3. Piping...

Beat further still till stiff peaks form - when you lift the beater blades the icing does not drop but forms spikes.

FROZEN WHIPPING CREAM

Rich's cream is a frozen whipping cream. The best cream for icing! This is soya cream, much lower in calories than dairy creams. It has a shelf life of 1 year in the freezer. It has sugar in it, and some flavour also added to it. Very easy to whip and gives much greater volume when whipped. To use, scrape out the amount you need from the carton into a bowl. Return carton back to the freezer immediately till further use. Thaw the cream in the bowl in the refrigerator or at room temperature till no ice crystals remain. Beat with an electric beater till you get the desired consistency.

- 1½ cups Rich's cream, fully thawed till it become like thin cream with no ice crystals (should still be very cold)
- 2 tbsp powdered sugar. Beat together cream and sugar till thick. Add flavouring ingredients as desired and beat again till thick.

TETRA PACK CREAMS

Amul and Vijaya cream come into this category. These are stabilized dairy creams. No fear of the cream turning into butter while beating. But since it is not a whipping cream, it sometimes becomes difficult to beat it till the peak stage. So for icing, keep the tetrapack in the fridge for 2 hours for the liquid to settle down. (Never keep in the freezer.) Cut the pack fully from the top and gently discard the liquid which generally settles at the bottom. Transfer the thick cream in a beating bowl and keep in the freezer for about 1 hour.

- 2 cups Amul or Vijaya Cream (chill without shaking the pack, take only thick part, discard any water content)
- ½ cup powdered sugar

Beat thick tetra pack cream on medium speed till thick. Only after it turns thick, then add sugar and continue beating on high speed till you get the desired consistency.

FRESH DAIRY CREAM

Avoid fresh dairy cream as far as possible. It turns into butter or curdles if not handled carefully. Transfer the cream in a beating bowl and keep in the freezer for about 1 hour.

- 2 cups Fresh Dairy Cream
- ½ cup icing sugar

Take a wide bowl filled with ice and put the bowl of cream on ice. Add icing sugar, essence and colour. Start beating cream at medium speed till it starts to get thick. Now reduce speed and beat till quite thick and soft peaks form. For piping, discard beaters and beat gently with a spoon till firm peaks are ready.

GLACE ICING

- 185 gms icing sugar
- 1 tsp unsalted butter - softened
- 4–8 tsp milk or water
- food colouring

Sift the icing sugar into a bowl and stir in the butter and enough milk or water to make a thick paste. Colour the icing at this stage if necessary. Warm slightly in a microwave or by standing the bowl in a pan of hot water, until thick and pourable.

Use immediately to prevent a crust forming and pour over the cake while warm.

- **Citrus icing:** Use lemon or orange juice in place of the milk.
- **Chocolate icing:** Stir in 4 tsp sifted cocoa powder
- **Strawberry icing:** Stir in a little pink food colour and strawberry essence.
- **Passion fruit icing:** Use passion fruit pulp in place of the milk.

BUTTER CREAM

Makes enough to cover and fill a 9 inch round cake

INGREDIENTS
- 125 gms unsalted butter, softened
- 250 gms icing sugar - sifted, 2 tbsp boiling water
- 1½ tsp vanilla essence or the flavour of your choice, colour as required

METHOD
Beat the butter with electric beaters until light and fluffy. Gradually add the icing sugar, beating well after each addition. Add the water and beat well. Add essence and colour. For chocolate butter cream, instead of essence and colour, add melted chocolate or sifted cocoa powder. Mix the chocolate or cocoa first with a little butter icing and then mix this to the total butter icing.

FLAVOURINGS FOR ICING

Mix whipped cream or butter with icing sugar till fluffy & of soft dropping consistency. To convert a plain icing to different flavours, do the following.

- **Chocolate:** Melt 4 tbsp chopped cooking chocolate and add 2 tbsp sifted cocoa powder and 4 tbsp castor sugar. Add 2-3 tbsp whipped cream or butter into it and mix. Now add this chocolate icing into the total whipped cream or butter to get chocolate icing.

- **Coffee:** Mix 2 tsp coffee powder in 1 tbsp hot water. Add 4 tbsp castor sugar. Add this to whipped cream or butter.

- **Strawberry, Mango, Orange or Pineapple:** Add ½ cup of any flavoured crush to whipped cream or butter, add colour if needed.

- **Butterscotch:** Add 2 tsp butterscotch essence and some yellow colour to whipped cream or butter.

CAKE STENCILS

1. This easy cake decoration is very effective for cakes. Cut strips of waxed paper and lay on the cake, some at angles. Sift powdered sugar over and carefully lift off the paper.

2. Paper doilies give round cakes an interesting finish. Place the doily on the cake and dust powdered sugar thickly through a sieve. For children's party cakes, animal shapes can be cut out of waxed paper and placed on the cake before powdered sugar is sifted over.

3. Lift off the paper doily leaving sugar decoration on the cake. With a little imagination, many messages and designs can be cut out of paper for cakes decorated this way.

| STEP 1 | STEP 2 | STEP 3 |

ALMOND ROSES

- 25 almonds - blanch, peel and dry
- 3 tbsp icing sugar
- 2-3 drops sweet almond essence
- raspberry red, green colour

METHOD
For the roses

1. Grind almonds. Add icing sugar and essence and knead it to a dough. If need be, add a few drops of water to make a firm, smooth dough. Knead well with your palm on a flat surface for about 6-8 minutes till a smooth dough is obtained and almond leaves its oil. The surface turns shiny.

2. Roll out small balls on a surface sprinkled with icing sugar. Cut into 2 pieces. Roll out each to get 2 centres.

3. Roll out more balls and cut. Arrange as petals around the centre. Turn edges to make a rose.

4. For leaves, make balls and roll them into long and pointed rolls. Flatten to make leaves and mark veins with a knife. Twist the leaf slightly.

STEP 1   STEP 2   STEP 3

STEP 4   STEP 4

CLASSIC VANILLA CAKE

For your convenience, two sizes of this cake are given below – 1 kg and ½ kg cakes. The use of cornflour gives its own distinctive texture. This is the cake you can rely on every time.

INGREDIENTS

- 1 tin condensed milk (400 gms)
- 1 cup milk, approx.
- 1 cup oil
- 6 tbsp powdered sugar
- 2 cups flour (maida)
- ½ cup cornflour
- 1 tsp soda-bicarb (mitha soda)
- 2 tsp level baking powder
- ½ cup soda water (a bottle of soda)
- 2 tsp vanilla essence
- a big baking tin of 10-11" diameter - lined with paper and greased

METHOD

1. Sift flour with cornflour, soda-bicarb and baking powder. Keep aside.
2. Mix sugar and condensed milk. Beat till light. Add oil. Beat well to mix.
3. Add half of the flour and half the milk. Mix well with a wooden spoon. Add essence. Add the remaining flour and the milk mixing well after the addition. Pour soda water and mix quickly.
4. Immediately pour batter in the prepared tin. Bake for 60 minutes in a preheated oven at 150°C.

INGREDIENTS

- ½ tin condensed milk (200 gms)
- ½ cup milk, approx.
- ½ cup oil
- 3 tbsp powdered sugar
- 1 cup flour (maida)
- ¼ cup cornflour
- ½ tsp soda-bicarb (mitha soda)
- 1 tsp baking powder
- ¼ cup soda water
- 1 tsp vanilla essence
- a medium baking tin of 7-8" diameter - lined with paper and greased

METHOD

1. Sift flour with cornflour, soda-bicarb and baking powder. Keep aside.
2. Mix sugar and condensed milk. Beat till light. Add oil. Beat well to mix.
3. Add half of the flour and half the milk. Mix well with a wooden spoon. Add essence. Add the remaining flour and the milk mixing well after the addition. Pour soda water and mix quickly.
4. Immediately pour batter in the prepared tin. Bake for 40 minutes in a preheated oven at 150°C.

TRUFFLE CAKE

A spectacular 3-layerd cake filled with chocolate cream. The main feature is the luscious dark chocolate and cream ganache that is poured over the top. Learn to make your own decorations and enjoy the oohs! and aahs! from your friends!

INGREDIENTS

- 1 chocolate cola cake, given on page 21 - baked in an 10" round tin or a square tin
- 200 gms whipping cream, preferably dairy or Rich's

SUGAR SYRUP TO SOAK

- 1/3 cup sugar and ¾ cup water, 1½ tbsp cocoa powder

GANACHE FOR TRUFFLE ICING

- 200 gms cream, preferably Amul
- 225 gms dark cooking chocolate - chopped (2¼ cups)
- 1 tsp butter

METHOD

1. Make a chocolate cola cake. Make sugar syrup by boiling water and sugar together. After the boil, keep syrup on low heat for 2-3 minutes to get a slightly sticky syrup. Add cocoa powder. Remove from heat and cool completely. Keep in the fridge.

2. To make ganache for truffle icing, heat 200 gms cream in a heavy bottom pan on low heat till it becomes hot. Do not let it boil. Add 225 gms chocolate to it. Mix nicely to remove any lumps. Remove from fire when almost melted and mix well with a rubber spatula. Add butter. Keep aside.

3. Beat 200 gms whipping cream till stiff peaks form.

4. Mix about ½ cup ganache from step 2, to the whipped cream to get a light brown chocolate cream. Keep chocolate cream in the fridge. Keep remaining ganache aside for top coating, outside the fridge, so that the chocolate remains melted.

5. Thinly remove the top layer of the cake. Cut chocolate cake into 3 layers.

6. Put a layer of cake on a plate, soak lightly with syrup. Spread ¼ of the prepared chocolate cream on it. Place the second layer of cake on it. Soak with 1/3 cup of syrup, using a spoon. Spread some chocolate cream on it. Place the top layer of cake on it. Again soak with 1/3 cup syrup.

7. Trim the sides. Cover the top and sides of the cake with the remaining chocolate cream. Keep it in the freezer for 15-20 minutes, till cream becomes firm.

8. Keep cake on a rack. Place a plate under the rack. Check ganache. The ganache can be reheated with 1-2 tbsp water, if it has become too thick. It should be thin enough to flow properly. Pour the prepared ganache on the set cake and tilt rack to cover the sides of the cake also.

9. Decorate sides with chocolate shards, given on page 58, placing them a little higher than the cake at an angle and curved sticks on the top in the centre.

TRUFFLE CAKE

TRUFFLE CAKE (continued)

INGREDIENTS FOR CHOCOLATE DECORATIONS
- 50-75 gms chocolate - chopped

METHOD
1. Chop chocolate and put in a microwave for 1½ minutes till soft. Stir with a rubber spatula to get it to a melted form.
2. For shards, quickly spread melted chocolate on butter paper/white paper in a thin layer. Keep in the fridge to set.
3. Remove from fridge and remove from paper.
4. Break into uneven shapes.
5. For sticks in the centre, put melted chocolate in a paper cone and pipe thick lines in a zig-zag fashion or nets on paper. Keep in the fridge to set. Remove from fridge and remove from paper. You can also use white chocolate in the same way. Keep these chocolate decorations in the fridge for 1-2 hours for them to become firm before using.

STEP 2

STEP 3

STEP 4

STEP 5

TWIN FLAVOUR CAKE

Strawberries and pineapple are used in this luscious gateaux, but can easily be substituted with other fruit combinations of your choice.

INGREDIENTS

- One recipe 1 kg vanilla cake
- 400 gms (2 cups) cream
- ½ cup strawberry crush
- ½ cup pineapple crush
- few drops of pink and lemon yellow colour, optional
- 1 cup pineapple syrup
- 2 slices tinned pineapple - drained and chopped

GARNISH

- strawberries
- ½ cup sugar
- ¼ cup water
- 1 tsp liquid glucose

METHOD

1. Make a classic vanilla cake of 1 kg, baked in an 10" round cake tin as given on page 55.
2. For the icing, beat cream till soft peaks form. Add strawberry crush and pink color to 1/3 of cream. Mix pineapple crush and lemon color to remaining cream and mix till thick. Keep in the fridge.
3. Cut cake into 4 equal layers. Lay the top layer on the platter, top side down. Soak with ¼ cup pineapple syrup.
4. Spread little less than half of pink cream on the first cake layer.
5. Place middle layer of cake over this. Soak with ¼ cup of syrup. Spread 1/3 of yellow cream on 2nd layer of cake and sprinkle chopped pineapple on cream.
6. Arrange 2nd middle layer of cake on top of the cake. Soak with syrup again.
7. Spread with strawberry cream, reserving about 1/3 cup for piping.
8. Arrange last layer of cake with the bottom side up. Soak again.
9. Cover the cake completely with cream on all sides and the top, reserving ½ cup for piping. Level top and sides with a broad knife dipped in chilled water.
10. Pipe strawberry cream and pineapple cream on cake with star and ribbon nozzle as shown in picture.
11. Halve big strawberries after washing and hulling them. Heat water. Add sugar and simmer till sugar dissolves and you get a sticky syrup. Add liquid glucose and stir to melt it. Add strawberries and stir gently to coat in syrup. Remove from syrup. Cool. Arrange on cake as shown in the picture.

CAPPUCCINO HAZELNUT CAKE

Serves 14-16

Discerning taste buds will appreciate the richness of hazelnut contrasted with dark coffee. It is easy to make though it looks complicated.

INGREDIENTS

- a cappuccino cake baked in a round tin of 7" diameter, page 29

COFFEE SYRUP FOR SOAKING

- 3 tsp coffee powder
- ¼ cup brown sugar
- ¾ cup water

ICING

- 200 gms whipping cream (Rich's cream)
- 3 tbsp cheese spread or cream cheese
- ¾ cup icing sugar, or to taste
- 5 tsp coffee powder mixed in 3-4 tsp hot water
- 4 tbsp chocolate hazelnut paste (ready made) - microwave if hard
- ferrero rocher chocolate
- dark chocolate cookies
- munchies and chocolate chips to decorate
- 1 tbsp cocoa - to sift on top

METHOD

1. Bake a cake as given on page 29 till step 7.
2. For soaking, boil water and sugar on low heat for 2-3 minutes till sugar melts. Remove from heat. Add coffee. Keep aside.
3. For icing, whip cream till soft peaks form. Keep aside. In a separate bowl, beat the cheese spread or cream cheese with sugar till smooth. Add coffee dissolved in water. Fold this into the whipped cream with a spatula. Put some in a piping bag.
4. To assemble, level the top of the cake if needed. Cut cake into 3 layers. Keep one layer on a serving platter. Soak with ½ of the cooled syrup.
5. Spread ¼ of the coffee flavoured icing.
6. Put some hazelnut paste on the second layer of cake and invert on the cake spread with icing.
7. Soak cake again and spread icing. Spread hazelnut paste on the last layer of cake and invert on the cream icing. Soak again.
8. Spread coffee icing on top & sides. Level with a palette knife dipped in a tall glass of cold water.
9. Put cookies on the sides. Sift cocoa on the cake through a tea strainer. Pipe swirls with icing in the piping bag. Decorate with chocolate chips, ferrero rocher and munchies.

CAPPUCCINO HAZLENUT CAKE

PINEAPPLE CHERRY CAKE

PINEAPPLE CHERRY CAKE

A spectacular 3-layerd cake filled with pineapples and cherries. The pineapple jam adds a delicious flavour to the cake.

PINEAPPLE CAKE
- ½ tin condensed milk (200 gms)
- ½ cup oil
- ½ tsp vanilla essence, ½ tsp pineapple essence
- ½ tsp soda-bicarb (*mitha soda*)
- a drop of yellow colour
- 1 tsp baking powder, 1¼ cups flour (*maida*)
- 3 tbsp powder sugar
- 2 slices tinned pineapple - very finely chopped
- ½ cup pineapple syrup

ICING
- 1¼ cup (250 gms) cream
- 4 tbsp powdered sugar
- 1 tsp pineapple essence
- 2 slices tinned pineapple - finely chopped
- 1 cup tinned cherries, remove seeds
- 3 tbsp pineapple jam - mix well with a tsp water till smooth

METHOD
1. To prepare the cake, line & grease an 8" round cake tin. Sift flour with soda-bi-carb & baking powder. Beat condensed milk & sugar. Add oil, colour & essence. Beat well. Add half of the flour and half the syrup. Mix well with a wooden spoon. Add the remaining flour and the syrup.
2. Mix chopped pineapple with 1 tbsp flour. Add to the cake batter and fold in with a spoon. Transfer the batter in the prepared container. Bake at 150°C for 40 minutes. Let it cool. Cut the cake into three layers.
3. For the icing, whip chilled cream with sugar and essence until thick and soft peaks form. Fill some in an icing gun and keep in the fridge.
4. Place the first layer of cake in a serving platter. Soak with ¼ cup of pineapple or cherry syrup till the cake feels moist. Spread 2 heaped tbsp cream. Top with half of the tinned cherries and pineapple. Spread pineapple jam on the second layer of cake and invert it over the cream. Press gently. Soak this layer of cake also. Spread 2 heaped tbsp cream and fruit again on the cake. Put jam on the third layer of cake and invert on the cream. Soak again with about ¼ cup syrup. Put remaining cream and spread gently to cover it completely on the top and sides.
5. Pipe a border with the cream in the icing gun using a star nozzle. Pipe lines on the sides also. Make swirls on top. Decorate with cherries and pineapple.

ITALIAN GATEAU

Serves 16-18

Follow these step-by-step instructions to create a magical web effect with icing, on a cake which has the most perfect combination of flavours – chocolate, vanilla and strawberry.

INGREDIENTS

- 1 kg vanilla cake, see page 55
- 250 gms (1¼ cups) whipping cream
- 3 tbsp cocoa, or to taste, ½-1 tsp vanilla essence
- 5-6 tbsp strawberry crush
- 100 gms cooking chocolate, to make curls
- some chocolate chips, optional

SUGAR SYRUP

- 1/3 cup sugar boiled with ¾ cup water for 2-3 minutes

STEP 7

METHOD

1. With a peeler, scrape the chocolate at room temperature on a plate so that about 1½ cup curls scatter on the plate. Do not touch them. Keep the curls in the freezer for 1-2 hours to get hard and frozen. See page 90.

2. Beat cream till stiff peaks form. Divide into 2 portions, making it 1/3 and 2/3. Mix cocoa in about 3 tbsp of water and add to the smaller portion (1/3 quantity) of cream to get a light brown colour and convert it into chocolate cream. Add just enough cocoa to get a nice brown colour. Do not make it too dark. Add vanilla essence to the remaining 2/3 portion of cream.

3. Make two butter paper cones and fill each with chocolate and vanilla cream separately. Keep the remaining icings for the cake.

4. Cut the cake into 3 layers. Place a layer of cake on a platter. Soak layer with 5-6 tbsp sugar syrup. Spread 3-4 heaped tbsp vanilla cream. Spread crush on the second layer of cake and invert over the cream. Soak this layer of cake also. Spread all the chocolate cream on it.

5. Spread crush on the last layer of cake and invert on the sandwiched cake. Soak the top layer of cake lightly. Cover top with vanilla cream. Cover sides also with vanilla cream. Level cream with a palette knife. Dip knife in cold water each time you level the cream.

6. With cones, draw circles of alternate colours, starting from the centre. Starting from the centre, pipe circles very close, leaving no gap between the two colours. Do this till half the cake is covered. Now pipe circular lines at ¼" intervals or slightly more, increasing the gap as you move towards the outer border. Alternately, draw line of both colours across the cake and then run toothpick in opposite direction as shown.

7. Run a toothpick across the circles from centre to the end in one direction. Now in the gaps between the two impressions, run the toothpick in the opposite direction to get a feather effect.

8. Arrange a row of chocolate chips at the edges. Decorate with bigger chocolate curls in the centre. With a palette knife, stick the remaining curls on the sides.

ITALIAN GATEAU

GERMAN CHOCOLATE
BLUEBERRY CAKE

GERMAN BLUEBERRY CAKE

This cake looks like a work of art – fresh vivid colours of fruit against a background that is chocolate brown and blueberry blue.

INGREDIENTS

- 1 chocolate cola cake, as on page 21
- 1¼ cups tinned blueberry topping and 2 tsp cornflour, see note
- 50 gms (½ cup) chopped dark chocolate - melted
- 60 gms (1/3 cup) sugar boiled with ¾ cup water for 2-3 minutes
- 250 gms (1¼ cup) whipping cream
- ¼ cup chopped white chocolate, for making nets, (page 58, step 5)
- black grapes and strawberries, optional

METHOD

1. For the cake, make batter by following the recipe on page 21. Transfer batter into an 9" square tin, which is lined with paper & greased. Bake at 150° C for 60 minutes. Check with tooth pick.

2. For blueberry topping, mix 2 tsp cornflour in ¼ cup water. Cook till it becomes thick. Remove from fire. Add 2-3 tbsp berry topping and mix gently. Add the remaining blueberry topping and stir gently to mix. You can also make home made topping as given below.

3. Beat cream at medium speed until thick. Put about 1 cup whipped cream in the icing gun. Keep aside. Melt ½ cup dark chocolate for 30 seconds in a microwave or on a double boiler. Keep aside.

4. Cut the cake into 3 layers. Place a layer of the cake on a serving platter. Spread melted chocolate on it with a palette knife. Keep in the fridge for 10 minutes for the chocolate to set.

5. Spread some berry topping on the chocolate. Place 2nd layer of cake on it. Soak with ¼ cup sugar syrup. Spread cream on top. Place the last layer of cake. Soak again. Spread cream on top and sides.

6. Make big swirls joining to each other on the edges with cream, forming a border all around. Keep in the fridge to set.

7. Fill the centre with berry topping. Melt white chocolate for 30 seconds in a microwave. Add 2-3 drops oil and stir to get a flowing consistency. Make nets as given on page 58. Decorate with nets and fresh fruits.

Home made Berry Topping

Mix ¾ cup black raisins in 1 cup (200 ml) grape juice and keep on fire. Dissolve 3 tsp cornflour in ½ cup water and add to the boiling raisins. Stir on low heat till thick. Add 2-3 tbsp strawberry or mixed fruit jam. Add some raspberry red colour if needed. Cool and use. Omit step 2.

NOUGAT CAKE WITH FRESH FRUITS

Serves 8

Learn how to make praline which is caramelised sugar that is allowed to set. Nuts are set in it, then roughly crushed and used as topping on any cake or dessert. In this cake it is used along with whipped cream and fresh fruit – an amazing new cake experience.

INGREDIENTS

CAKE

- 1 ¼ cups yogurt, 2 tbsp lemon juice
- 90 gms (½ cup) salted butter
- 100 gms (¾ cup) powdered sugar
- 200 gms (1¾ cups) flour (*maida*)
- 2 tsp baking powder
- 1 tsp soda-bicarb
- ¼ cup milk

ICING

- 200 gms whipping cream
- 1 tsp butterscotch essence
- ¼ cup sugar boiled with ½ cup water for soaking

PRALINE

- ½ cup regular sugar
- ¼ cup roasted peanuts

COLOURED FRESH FRUITS

- 1 bright red apple
- 1 malta or orange
- 1 tinned pineapple slice
- 1 kiwi
- a few cherries, strawberries

MIRROR GEL FOR COATING FRUITS

- 2 tbsp sugar
- ¼ cup water
- 1 tsp liquid glucose

METHOD

1. For the cake, line a 9½" x 4½" tube cake tin (big loaf tin) with paper. Grease paper and sides. Preheat oven to 190°C/375°F.

2. Sieve flour, baking powder and soda-bicarb together. Keep aside. Beat sugar and butter very well. Mix yogurt and lemon juice. To the beaten sugar and butter, fold in sieved flour alternately with yogurt and lemon juice mixture. Mix. Do not over mix or beat. Add milk and mix gently. Put immediately in the greased tin and bake in the preheated oven for 30 minutes or till the cake is done.

3. Whip cream with essence till firm peaks are formed. Refrigerate till use.

4. For praline on the sides, put sugar in a non stick pan. Spread out in a flat layer covering the bottom of the pan. Keep on medium heat for 2-3 minutes without touching the sugar. When the sugar starts to turn golden, remove from fire and swirl the pan lightly till the sugar melts completely. Return to fire. Wait till sugar caramelizes and turns light golden. Pour some designs on the greased kitchen platform with 2-3 tbsp of caramel sugar to form praline shards as shown on the next page. To the remaining caramelized sugar in the pan, add the nuts. Pour on a greased kitchen platform. Let it cool and then crush roughly for the cake.

5. Cut cake into 2 layers. Place one layer of cake on the serving plate. Soak with 4-5 tbsp sugar syrup. Put 2-3 tbsp heaped cream and spread gently. Sprinkle some praline. Apply cream on the second layer of cake and invert on the praline. Press. Soak lightly with syrup.

Contd...

NOUGAT CAKE WITH FRESH FRUITS

6. Cover with cream on the top. Level top with a palette knife dipped in cold water. Cream the sides also. Make a shell border on the edges with the small star nozzle. Refrigerate.

7. Cut fruits decoratively as leaves, fans and baskets as given on next page. Make apple leaves. Cut orange slices with the peel on. You can make 2 baskets from a kiwi by cutting through the center in a "V" style. Flatten the base of the kiwi basket. Cut pineapple slice into small pieces and fill the blank spaces on the cake with them. Strawberries can be made into fans also.

8. For shine on the fruits, prepare mirror gel. Boil sugar and water together in a small pan. Simmer for 5 minutes till it turns syrupy and of one thread consistency. Add liquid glucose to the sugar syrup and mix well. Remove from fire. Keep aside to brush on fruits.

9. Remove cake from fridge. Stick praline on the sides.

10. Decorate top with fruits. Brush fruits with the prepared mirror gel. Arrange praline shards.

PRALINE SHARDS WITH CARAMELIZED SUGAR

- ¼ cup regular sugar
- a small flat pan, oil for greasing

1. Grease the kitchen platform with some oil.

2. Put sugar in a flat pan or a non stick pan. Spread out in a flat layer covering the bottom of the pan. Keep on medium heat for 2-3 minutes without touching the sugar. When the sugar starts to turn golden at the edges, reduce heat and stir just once gently from the edges. Wait till it turns light golden. Do not make it too golden.

3. Immediately, with a spoon pour out flowers, leaves or abstract design on the greased platform. Make more sugar shards. Let them cool.

4. Gently remove from the platform.

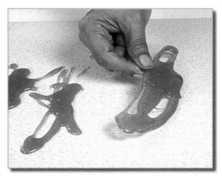

STEP 3   STEP 4

APPLE LEAF

1. Halve an unpeeled, red apple. (Leave the core in the apple.) Place the apple half cut side down. Using a sharp knife, cut a 1½" long, narrow, V-shaped piece out of the middle to get a small boat shaped piece. (step 1) Keep it aside.

2. Follow the lines of the first boat and cut out another, larger V-shaped piece at an angle to get a bigger boat shape. Keep the knife a little tilted while cutting. Repeat this process 2-3 more times (step 2). Keep all the pieces aside. Sprinkle some lemon juice on the cut surfaces.

3. Place the first small piece inverted, with skin side up on the second boat, keeping it a little higher from the end, so that both the pieces show nicely.

4. Arrange the two boats on the third, keeping it a little higher so that all three together look like a leaf. (step 4)

| STEP 1 | STEP 2 | STEP 3 | STEP 4 |

STRAWBERRY FAN

1. Choose firm, ripe, red strawberries. Place strawberry, pointed end up, on a board and make cuts in the berry, taking care not to slice all the way through. The number of cuts depends on the size of the strawberry - 4 for small berries and 8 for larger ones.

2. Hold the strawberry gently and twist in the opposite direction so that the slices fan out. With the point of a knife carefully cut out the green hull.

3. Replace the hull with a sprig of fresh mint.

| STEP 1 | STEP 2 | STEP 3 |

BLACK FOREST CAKE

Serves 16

This famous cake draws attention with its contrasting colours – dark brown, snow white and cherry red. A 4-layerd cake, sandwiched with whipped cream – definitely a special occasion celebration.

INGREDIENTS

- 1 chocolate cola cake, page 21
- 1 tin of cherries
- 1 tbsp rum
- 100 gms (1 cup) dark chocolate - for the curls

CREAM ICING

- 400 gms (2 cups) cream - chilled
- powdered sugar to taste
- 1 tsp vanilla essence

STEP 8

STEP 9

METHOD

1. With the help of a vegetable peeler, start peeling the side of the chocolate slab on to a plate, applying a little pressure as you peel. The chocolate should neither be too cold nor too soft. Keep curls in the freezer for half an hour to harden. See page 94.

2. Grate some chocolate to get tiny curls for the sides. Keep the curls spread out in a plate in the freezer.

3. Beat cream till thick. Add sugar and essence and beat carefully till the cream is very thick and can stand in soft peaks. Put some in an icing bag or gun and keep in the fridge. Keep the rest of the cream also in the fridge.

STEP 10

4. Remove seeds from 1 cup cherries. Keep aside. Add rum or essence to 1 cup cherry syrup.

5. Cut the cake into 4 layers. Place a cake layer on a serving platter. Soak with ¼ cup cherry syrup. Spread some cream icing on cake.

6. Put deseeded cherries on the cream. Cover these with the other layer of cake.

7. Soak cake again with ¼ cup syrup. Repeat with the remaining layers of cake and cream, keeping 1½ cups cream for the top and sides. Cover the cake completely with cream on all sides and the top. Level top and sides with a broad knife dipped in chilled water.

8. Make a border on the edge by closely piping swirls of cream from the icing gun. For the lower border, hold the piping bag at such an angle that half the swirl is on the cake and the other half of the swirl is on the platter.

9. Place cherries on swirls. Put big curls on the top. Stick the tiny curls on the sides with a flat spoon.

10. If you like, make shards of chocolate as given on page 58 and write a message with melted white chocolate put in a paper cone. Refrigerate.

BLACK FOREST CAKE

CHOCOLATE FUDGE CAKE
WITH ROASTED NUTS

CHOCOLATE FUDGE CAKE WITH ROASTED NUTS

Serves 10-12

A thick and rich ganache (dark chocolate and cream cooked together) is the generous filling as well as the topping of this extravagant cake. Roasted nuts provide depth and contrast.

INGREDIENTS

- a dark chocolate cake, as given on page 16
- a baking tin of 7-8" diameter - line bottom with paper and grease paper and sides

OTHER INGREDIENTS

- ¼ cup sugar, 1½ tbsp cocoa powder and ¾ cup water - boil and simmer for 2 minutes, for soaking
- ¼ cup chopped almonds
- ¼ cup chopped walnuts - roasted on low heat
- ½ cup (100 gms) cream
- 1½ cups chopped dark chocolate (150 gms)
- ¼-½ rounded tsp liquid glucose (warm in a microwave if too hard)
- ficus leaves, optional

STEP 3

STEP 4

METHOD

1. Make the cake in a 7" round cake tin. Cut the top of the cake to level it and collect the crumbs for the roses if you like. Cake trimmings make beautiful roses as shown in picture of the cake.

2. For roses, add liquid glucose to about ½ cup cake trimmings and mix well to get a smooth pliable dough. Make roses with this chocolate dough as given for almond roses on page 54.

3. Melt 2 tbsp chocolate in a microwave or a double boiler as given on page 15 till soft. Stir with a spoon till well melted. Brush on washed ficus leaves or spread with a spoon on the leaves on the right side. Keep in the fridge to set.

4. Very carefully peel the leaf off the chocolate, starting at the stem end. Keep chocolate leaves in the freezer for 1-2 hours to become hard.

5. For the topping, warm cream in a pan. Add remaining chopped chocolate and stir till smooth. Stir on low heat till smooth to form ganache. Remove from fire. Keep ganache aside.

6. Cut the cake into two layers. Place one layer of cake on a rack. Keep an empty plate beneath it. Soak cake with 5-6 tbsp cocoa and sugar syrup. Pour some chocolate ganache on it. Place the second layer of cake on it. Soak again. Pour the remaining chocolate ganache on it to cover top and sides completely.

7. Sprinkle the almonds and walnuts on the cake to cover completely.

8. Collect the chocolate ganache from the plate beneath the rack and put in a small pan. Add 1-2 tbsp water and stir on low heat to get a pouring consistency. Put in a paper cone and pipe lines very closely on the nuts placed on the cake. Arrange 3 roses on a side and chocolate leaves around them.

GUITAR CAKE

Two cakes, one long and one square, are needed to make the guitar shape. A two-colour scheme, with fine lines of brown on white, give this cake an elegant look, created with white butter icing and chocolate ganache.

INGREDIENTS
- 2 recipes of dark chocolate cake, page 16, bake one in a big loaf tin (10" × 5") and one in a square cake tin (8" × 8")
- 50 gms chocolate – for piping lines

CHOCOLATE GANACHE ICING ON THE CAKE
- 300 gm cream
- 350 gms chocolate - cut into small pieces (3½ cups)
- I tbsp butter, 2 tbsp powdered sugar

BUTTER ICING (WHITE)
- 150 gms (I cup) unsalted white butter, softened
- 300 gms (3 cups) icing sugar, 2 tbsp boiling water
- 2 tsp vanilla essence, 4 drops lemon juice

METHOD
1. First trim the loaf for the neck of the guitar, from the length side by 1" and diagonally cut the end to shape the end of the guitar.
2. Shape the square cake like the bottom of the guitar.
3. Place the long cake joining the centre above of the square.
4. To make the chocolate ganache – heat the cream with sugar in a pan and immediately add the chocolate pieces to it. Stir well with a wooden spoon so that it softens. Remove from fire and add butter. Mix well till it turns smooth and blends well. Pour the warm ganache over the cake, such that it flows from the sides and covers the sides also. Let it cool in the refrigerator to set.
5. Butter icing – beat the butter with an electric beater until light and fluffy. Gradually add icing sugar, beating well after each addition. Add water and beat well. Add essence, if need be add 2-3 tsp of hot water.
6. Make 2 paper cones and fill each with some butter icing and keep in the fridge. Keep the remaining in the bowl also in the refrigerator.
7. Once the chocolate ganache is set, mark the centre brown portion with a tooth pick. Cut a thick tip in a paper cone and pipe a white border around the chocolate portion.
8. Spread the white butter icing on the remaining part of the guitar to cover it nicely. Level with a flat knife dipped in hot water. Pipe thickly on the edges with the white icing paper cone.
9. Melt 50 gms chocolate on a double boiler and put this also in a paper cone. Cut the other white icing cone to get thin lines and draw the lines with melted chocolate and thin white icing to make it appear like guitar strings as shown in the picture.

GUITAR CAKE

MIDNIGHT FANTASY

Follow the steps carefully and wait for the applause. A very professional looking confection, worth the time spent on decorating it. The chocolate collar comes out very well if you have practiced henna (mehandi) designs.

INGREDIENTS

- Chocolate cola cake baked in 10" tin as given on page 21 or a cappuccino cake as given on page 29 baked in a 8" cake tin
- 150 gms (1½ cups) dark cooking chocolate - at room temp
- 75 gms white cooking chocolate - chopped
- 300 gms cream, ½ cup icing sugar, 1 tsp vanilla essence
- a few chocolate thins, optional

TO SOAK

- ¾ cup water
- ¼ cup sugar, 2 tsp coffee

METHOD

1. With a peeler, scrape sides of the cooking chocolate slab which should neither be chilled nor melting, to get 10-15 large curls, as given on page 90. Chop the remaining chocolate.

2. Whip cream till thick. Add icing sugar and essence and beat till stiff peaks form. Divide into 3 portions. Fill one portion in an icing bag. Keep aside 2nd portion also plain white for topping. The last portion is converted to choco cream for sandwiching the cake in the next step.

3. Soften the chopped chocolate in a microproof bowl for 40 seconds. Stir to melt it nicely. Add half of the melted chocolate to last part of whipped cream to get choco-cream. Keep the remaining half of the melted chocolate for the collar.

4. Level the top of the cake. Cut the cake into 3 layers. Boil water, sugar for 2 minutes. Add coffee and remove from fire. Soak first layer of cake with 1/3 of this black coffee. Spread half of choco-cream. Repeat till you put the last layer of cake. Soak again. Spread the top of the cake with plain white cream. Lightly spread some cream also on the sides of the cake for the collar. Pipe an outer border of swirls with white cream with the icing bag. Pipe a second inner border too making semi circles on the cake, as shown.

5. For collar, measure the height of cake. Cut a strip of butter paper, wide and long enough to wrap around the cake. Draw a design on it with a pencil. Microwave white chocolate for 30 seconds to soften it and stir with a rubber spatula to melt it. Spoon in a butter paper cone.

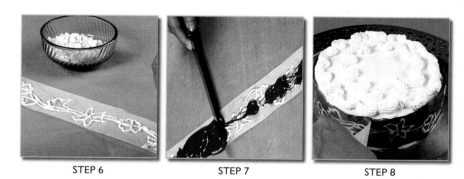

| STEP 6 | STEP 7 | STEP 8 |

6. Pipe on the drawn design on the paper strip and leave to set for 2 minutes. If the white chocolate sets in the cone while piping, microwave paper cone for 5-7 seconds to melt the white chocolate.

7. Melt dark chocolate again in the microwave for just 5-7 seconds and quickly spread it over the white design and the entire strip of paper with a palate knife.

8. Quickly wrap strip around the cream coated sides of the cake with the chocolate on the inside touching the cake. Do not over lap the ends of the paper. Leave in fridge for 5 minutes. Peel off the paper from the collar once the chocolate sets.

9. Arrange chocolate curls in the centre in a heap and thins on the swirls of cream on the outer border.

TRAIN CAKE

Two loaf-shaped cakes are used to make the shape of this charming train. Bright contrasting colours in the icing will thrill every youngster.

INGREDIENTS

- 2 vanilla cakes made in loaf tin 9" × 4" (each of ½ kg), page 55
- Food colours – blue, yellow and red
- 2-3 tbsp cocoa or ½ cup chopped chocolate
- wooden skewers or sticks, decorative candles

BUTTER ICING

- 150 gms (1 cup) unsalted white butter, softened
- 300 gms (3 cups) icing sugar
- 2 tbsp boiling water
- 2 tsp vanilla essence
- 4 drops lemon juice

METHOD

1. Cut the 1st loaf into two horizontally to get the base of the train.
2. Cut 1/3 part of the second cake and keep aside.
3. With the remaining 2/3 part, give it a cylindrical shape by cutting the end into a rounded shape as given in the picture. Just cut the sides also slightly to give it a rounded appearance like a cylinder.
4. Place the base loaf cake (one layer from the first cake) on a cake board. Put the cylinder cake horizontally on the base cake on one side so that you could pile the blocks (cut into squares) of the remaining cake from the remaining pieces. Cut two rounds with a cookie cutter to place on the top of the engine of the train.
5. Divide the butter icing into 5 bowls. Add colour to each bowl like red, yellow, blue, melted chocolate/cocoa to make brown. Keep some white also.
6. With a star nozzle first start with cocoa - make the base all over leaving blue colour for wheels. Then wash the piping bag, fill blue and pipe the blue part then red and lastly the yellow. Decorate with candles on the wooden sticks.

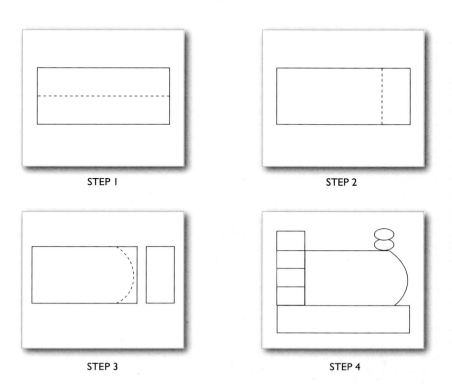

STEP 1

STEP 2

STEP 3

STEP 4

ALPHABET CAKE

Make this cake for your child on his/her birthday and make their day really special. If your child's name begins with any other alphabet - bake the cake in the swiss roll tin & cut out the desired alphabet from it.

INGREDIENTS

- 1 kg vanilla cake as given on page 55 - make cake in an 9" × 11" swiss roll, lined on the base and all sides with butter paper and greased well
- ½ cup mango juice mixed with ¼ cup water - for soaking cake

MANGO CREAM FOR SPREADING BETWEEN LAYERS OF CAKE

- 300 gms (1½ cups) heavy whipping cream (Rich's cream)
- 2-3 tbsp mango crush
- a few drops yellow color

DECORATIONS

- yellow and pink sugar paste or marzipan flowers
- yellow sugar vermicelli
- pink, yellow, orange and red jelly spirals
- One cake board or thick cardboard 11" x 13" covered with foil

METHOD

1. Beat cream till stiff peaks form. Divide into 4 parts. To one part, fold in mango crush. Keep the second part white and put in the piping bag. Mix the remaining 2 parts and add yellow colour to it to get a pale yellow icing for topping.
2. Cut cake into an "A" shape with the help of a knife. Slice the cake into two layers.
3. Place the base layer on the prepared board. Soak the base layer with some mango juice and water mixture.
4. Spread the mango crush-cream on the base layer.
5. Place the top layer of the cake on the mango cream filling.
6. Soak the top layer also with the remaining mango juice and water mixture.
7. Spread the firmly beaten lemon coloured cream all over the cake (on the top and all sides). Smoothen the cream with a palette knife dipped in cold water.
8. Sprinkle coloured sugar vermicelli.
9. Pipe a border on the top and bottom edges of the cake with white icing in the piping bag. Arrange flowers and jelly spirals. Refrigerate till serving time.

ALPHABET CAKE

CAR CAKE

Two loaf-shaped cakes, one small and one big, are used to make this cute little car that will bring smiles to the faces of all the little toddlers.

INGREDIENTS

- 1 kg vanilla cake recipe made in 2 loaf tins, one small tin and one big loaf tin, page 55
- 2 tbsp jam
- 50 gms melted chocolate - melted and put in a paper cone
- 3-4 tbsp desiccated coconut
- some gems to decorate

FROSTING

- 125 gms (¾ cup + 2 tbsp) - unsalted butter softened
- 3 tbsp milk
- 250 gms (2½ cups) icing sugar – sifted
- 1 tsp strawberry essence
- 2-3 drops lemon juice
- raspberry red colour as required

METHOD

1. Take the smaller loaf cake. With a serrated knife, slice off one end at a sharp angle about 1" from the base for the back of car. Cut the other end at a less acute angle for the front of the car. The roof of the car should be rounded from the back. It should slant in front to look like a windscreen, then gradually slope in front for the bonnet.

2. Level the big loaf cake to get a height of about 2½". Cut roundels from the trimmings to form wheels. Place this 2½" loaf cake on the cake board. Spread with melted jam. Place the smaller loaf cake which is shaped like a car on it. Fix wheels on 4 corners with the help of tooth picks. Now finally trim it to shape it like the car shown in the picture.

3. Now prepare the frosting – melt butter and milk on low heat in a saucepan. Remove from fire when butter melts. Add lemon juice. Just add a drop of color and essence to it. Add icing sugar. Beat with an electric beater for 2-3 minutes until smooth. Pour warm on the cake on the top and tap cake lightly to coat. Let the icing fall on sides and coat the sides as well.

4. Quickly stick some desiccated coconut on the lower edge with a knife so that it sticks while the frosting sets. Let it cool.

5. When cool, melt the chocolate on a double boiler and put in a paper cone and make the outlines for windscreen, wheels and a smiley face on the bonnet. Decorate with gems as lights, using melted chocolate to stick.

BUTTERFLY CAKE

One large cake is cut according to the drawings below. Coloured jellies are used to fill the wings of the butterfly for a shiny, bright look that will delight the children.

INGREDIENTS
- 1 kg vanilla cake made in 10"-11" cake tin, page 55
- 400 gms whipping cream - dairy or rich's
- 5-6 tbsp powdered sugar (if using Rich's, no sugar is needed)
- 1 tsp butterscotch essence or vanilla essence
- 1 cup sugar syrup (¼ cup sugar + 1 cup water - boil together for 2 minutes and cool)

OTHER INGREDIENTS FOR THE BUTTERFLY
- packets of strawberry and lemon jelly
- some long candies for the centre of the butterfly
- some thousand island balls

PRALINE
- ¼ cup regular sugar
- 10-12 almonds - each broken into 2-3 pieces
- a small non stick pan
- oil for greasing

METHOD
1. To make the praline, grease the kitchen platform with some oil. Put sugar in a non stick pan. Spread out in a flat layer covering the bottom of the pan. Keep on medium heat for 2-3 minutes without touching the sugar. When the sugar starts to turn golden, reduce heat and stir just once gently from the edges. Wait till it turns light golden and it melts. Add almonds, mix and immediately pour on the greased platform. Cool. Remove and crush to a coarse powder with a rolling pin (belan). Store in an air tight box.
2. Prepare both jellies as per the instructions on the packet, but use ½ cup less water than given on the packet as we need a firm jelly for icing. Refrigerate the jellies.
3. Beat cream with sugar till fluffy. Add essence and beat till firm peaks form.
4. Line a cake board or the back of a tray with aluminium foil. Stick foil with jam to the tray on the back. Keep aside.
5. Cut cake into 2 halves. Place the bottom piece on a flat board. Soak with half cup sugar syrup.
6. Put cream generously and spread. Sprinkle the prepared praline. Place the second piece on it. Soak with syrup again.
7. Cut into the desired shape as shown in the sketches, by marking with a knife as shown in step b. Follow step c to cut the centre, follow step d to place the cut pieces turned out and finally follow step e to cut again. Join pieces as shown in step f. Arrange the pieces on the prepared board to make a butterfly.

BUTTERFLY CAKE

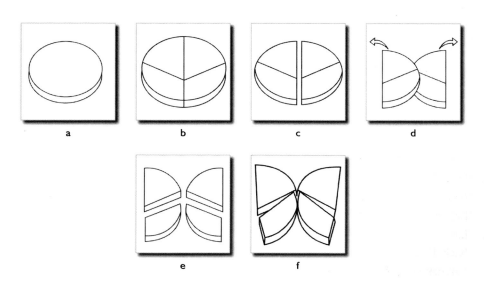

a   b   c   d

e   f

8. Cover the top and sides generously with cream. Level with a palette knife dipped in cold water. With cream, make the top border which helps to keep jelly in place. Chill cake in the freezer for 15-20 minutes before you do the jelly icing.

9. When jelly is semi-set, mix well and put jelly on the iced cake. Decorate with hundred thousand, gems etc. Keep the prepared cake in the fridge to set.

ANNIVERSARY TWO TIER CAKE

Serves 30

The cakes are soaked in coffee-cocoa syrup and layered with mocha cream icing to give a moist texture. A classy and sophisticated look is just right for the occasion.

INGREDIENTS
- 1 kg vanilla cake baked in an 11" round tin, page 55
- ½ kg vanilla cake baked in a 5" round tin, page 55

CREAM ICING
- 800 gms (4 cups) heavy whipping cream (Rich's cream) - whipped till soft peaks
- 25 gms (¼ cup chopped) chocolate - melted on a double boiler, page 10
- 2 tbsp cocoa
- 1 tbsp coffee

SUGAR SYRUP
- ½ cup sugar boiled with 1 cup water for 2 minutes
- 3 tbsp cocoa
- 1 tsp coffee

DECORATIONS
- almond roses as explained on page 54
- pink and yellow plastic ribbons
- coloured sugar vermicelli

METHOD
1. Mix melted chocolate with cocoa and coffee. Add to 1/3 of the whipped cream to make mocha cream. Keep the remaining white cream for topping.
2. Slice the large cake into two layers. Place the base layer on the board.
3. Add cocoa and coffee to sugar syrup. Soak the base layer with this sugar syrup. Spread a little more than half of the mocha cream on the base. Place the top layer of cake on the cream filling. Soak the top layer also with sugar syrup. Spread some white cream icing all over the cake. Smoothen the cream with a palette knife dipped in cold water.
4. Slice the smaller cake into two layers. Place the base of the smaller cake on the top centre of the larger cake. Similarly soak, spread mocha cream, top with the second layer. Soak again. Spread some white cream icing all over the small cake too. Smoothen the cream with a palette knife dipped in cold water.
5. Throw some vermicelli carefully on the sides.
6. Fit a piping bag with a star nozzle. Fill it with stiffly beaten white cream. Pipe a row of commas all around the base and top of both the cakes.
7. Place 2 flowers (one yellow rose, one pink rose) at 4 places on the large cake. Fit in ribbon loops into each bunch. Similarly put 3 bunches on the top cake. Sprinkle lots of silver balls on top.

ANNIVERSARY TWO TIER CAKE

MARZIPAN TOPPED CAKE

MARZIPAN TOPPED CAKE

The 3 layers of this cake are soaked in syrup then sandwiched with marmalade butter icing. It is totally covered with a smooth sheet of marzipan – simple yet gourmet quality.

INGREDIENTS

- ½ kg vanilla or malai cake as given on page 55 or page 20
- ¼ cup sugar boiled with ¾ cup water for 2 minutes, for soaking

MARZIPAN TOPPING

- 1/3 cup almonds - blanched
- 40 gms (1/3 cup) icing sugar
- 2½ tbsp grain sugar
- 2 tbsp water
- 1 tsp liquid glucose (microwave for a few seconds if hard)
- different colours - raspberry red, blue, green, yellow etc.

BUTTER ICING

- 50 gms (¼ + 1 tbsp) unsalted butter
- 100 gms (1 cup) icing sugar - sifted
- 1 tbsp very hot water
- 4 tbsp orange marmalade - whisked slightly
- ½ tsp vanilla essence
- 2 drops lemon juice

METHOD

1. For the marzipan topping, put almonds in 1 cup water and microwave for 1-2 minutes. Slip the skins off and pat dry with a paper napkin. Grid almonds and icing sugar in a grinder to a fine powder. Leave in the grinder.

2. Cook grain sugar and water is a small flat pan to a one string consistency. Check a drop of syrup between the thumb and finger to see that a thread is formed when they are pulled apart. Add liquid glucose to syrup. Mix.

3. Remove syrup from fire and immediately add hot syrup to almond-sugar mix in the grinder. Grind together to a paste. Remove marzipan to the kitchen platform. Knead for about 2-3 minutes to get a pliable dough. Divide dough into 2 portions, 1/3 and 2/3 quantity. Colour the bigger portion blue and keep the smaller portion white to colour later. Keep all covered in cling wrap.

4. To prepare butter icing, beat butter with electric beaters until light and fluffy. Gradually add the icing sugar, beating well. Add hot water and beat well. Add lemon juice and essence. Beat well. To ¼ cup of icing add 4 tbsp orange marmalade for sandwiching the cake. Keep remaining icing for the top.

5. Cut cake into 3 layers. Place a piece on a flat surface. Soak with 4-5 tbsp of sugar syrup. Spread some orange marmalade butter icing. Place the second layer of cake and soak again. Cover with the last layer of cake. Soak again. Top the sandwiched cake with plain butter icing, and on the sides also.

6. Roll out the blue marzipan dough on the kitchen platform dusted with icing sugar thinly. It should be bigger than the cake so as to cover the top and sides of the cake. Place on the cake spread with butter icing.

7. Colour the remaining dough as you like and make flowers. Stick using butter icing. Write the message with some butter icing filled in a paper cone.

RACING TRACK NUMBER 8

Young boys will be delighted to show off this racing track. Really worth the effort for your son's birthday party.

INGREDIENTS

- 2 round chocolate cola cake, each of 10-11" diameter, page 21
- 400 gms (2 cups) whipping cream, preferably Rich's cream
- 50 gms (½ cup) icing sugar, or to taste
- 2 tbsp cocoa powder
- 75 gms cooking chocolate - chopped (¾ cup)
- ½ cup desiccated coconut + few drops green colour- mixed together in a bowl
- ½ cup desiccated coconut + few drops orange-red color- mixed together in a bowl
- 1 cup milk + 1½ tbsp sugar - mix together
- 4-5 dark chocolate biscuits/cookies - finely crushed
- jellies, stone and gum candies
- 3 or 4 small racing cars
- 2 small paper flags made from wrapping paper with toothpicks and glue

CAKE BOARD (CHECK SIZE TO SEE THAT IT FITS INTO THE FRIDGE)

- 14"x14" card board (you can use an old carton), foil to cover, jam to brush

METHOD

1. Beat cream with icing sugar till thick and soft peaks form. Divide into 2 portions. Melt 50 gms chocolate in a double boiler. Remove from double boiler and add 2 tbsp cocoa to it. Mix well. Cool slightly and add to one portion of cream to get chocolate cream for sandwiching the cake. Keep one part white.

2. Trim both the cakes on one side, so that they can join well to form Number 8. Cut each piece into half horizontally. Place base layers on the board joining together.

3. Soak with milk. Spread chocolate cream on the base layers. Sprinkle the remaining chopped chocolate on the cream. Place top layers of cake on the cream, and soak with sweetened milk.

4. Spread stiffly beaten white cream on the top and sides.

5. Mark two small circles in the middle of both cakes with the help of a steel or plastic container of 4" diameter, placed on the cake. Sprinkle crushed cookies around the marked circles, on the outside to make the track.

6. Cover sides of the cake with orange coconut with a knife.

7. Sprinkle green coloured coconut inside both the marked circles on the white cream. Place jellies and candies on the cake. Place cars on the cookie area. For flags, cut triangles from paper and stick with glue on the toothpicks. Place flags as shown.

8. For the board, melt 2 tbsp jam and brush the foil lined board thinly with it. Sprinkle crushed cookies sparingly on it and outline board with green coconut. Place candies randomly.